fair shares for all

fair shares for all

A MEMOIR OF FAMILY AND FOOD

John Haney

RANDOM HOUSE | NEW YORK

Published in the United States by Random House,
an imprint of The Random House Publishing Group,
a division of Random House, Inc., New York.

RANDOM HOUSE and colophon are registered
trademarks of Random House, Inc.

All photos in this work are courtesy of the Haney family.

LIBRARY OF CONGRESS CATALOGING-IN-PUBLICATION DATA

Haney, John.
Fair shares for all : a memoir / John Haney.
p. cm.
ISBN 978-1-4000-6233-1
1. Haney family. 2. Haney, John, 1954—Family.
3. Working class—England—London—Biography.
4. Food. 5. London (England)—Biography. I. Title.
CT787.H36H36 2007
942.1085'5092—dc22   2006037622

Printed in the United States of America on acid-free paper

www.atrandom.com

2 4 6 8 9 7 5 3 1

FIRST EDITION

Book design by Barbara M. Bachman

This book is respectfully dedicated

to the memory of my parents,

DENIS *and* KITTY,

and to my sister,

JOY

Memory, memory,

what do you want with me?

—PAUL VERLAINE, "NEVERMORE,"

FROM *POÈMES SATURNIENS*

contents

PART ONE

a cliff face of stilton

1. A MONSTROUS BOWL OF PEANUTS
   IN THE SHELL   3

2. KIPPERS AND CUSTARD   29

3. BOTTOMLESS BUMPERS OF PORT   50

PART TWO

a nice cup of tea and a biscuit

4. A PIPSQUEAK OF MARMALADE   63

5. HIGH-SPEED BURNT TOAST
   AND FAKE COFFEE   88

6. THE HASTY CONSUMPTION
   OF PILCHARDS   100

7. COCOA AND CORNED BEEF SANDWICHES   114

8.   GREASY GRUB AND GLIDING   134

9.   THE BIRTHPLACE OF TOAD-IN-THE-HOLE   150

PART THREE

a splat or two of all-devouring mustard

10.   DAMAGE FROM OILY CHICKPEAS   167

11.   THE GRAYING PURVEYORS OF
        HADDOCK AND EELS   184

12.   A NONCONSOLATORY SPLURGE
        OF MEURSAULT   217

13.   DRIP-DRY SHIRTS, SPILT MILK,
        AND SUGARED ALMONDS   238

EPILOGUE
HAM AND CHEESE, EGG SALAD,
HAM SOLITAIRE   261

Author's Note   277
Acknowledgments   281

fair shares for all

PART ONE

· · · ·

a cliff face of stilton

The author at three weeks, March 1954

CHAPTER 1

A Monstrous Bowl of Peanuts in the Shell

. . . .

ONE SUNDAY MORNING IN OCTOBER 1959, MY FATHER, DENIS, informed me, while chewing a little morosely on a marmalade sandwich, that one of my aunt Rose's sisters—who, like Rose and her husband, Dad's half-brother, Don, lived in a part of London known as the Isle of Dogs—was getting married at the weekend. And "all of us," "the Haney mob" entire, had been invited.

At this news, I excitedly emitted, through a mouth stuffed with soldiers—toast slashed into fingers for dipping in soft-boiled eggs—a butter-blotted gasp of interest and approval. I'd been bewitched by the name of the place (and by the knowledge that the island concerned sat at the heart of the working-class East End, from which my father's side of the family came) ever since a very different Sunday some months earlier, when I'd first heard it mentioned, by Don himself, at the hospital bedside of my dying maternal grandmother. It was also on that Sunday that I'd first met "all of us" en masse, in fact, and, within minutes, grown not only to like them but to find myself feeling more at home in their company than I did with my parents.

My outburst, predictably, provoked a standard-issue, much-resented reprimand from Kitty, my wildly ambitious though not particularly educated mum. She came from the solidly lower-middle-class London borough of Redbridge, spoke with an accent that some of our Cockney relatives quite justifiably thought upper-crusty, and was, at that moment, otherwise engaged in retrieving the sleepy head of my three-year-old sister, Joy, from the hill fort of cornflakes into which it had fallen. I was, according to Mum, supposed to be eating my soldiers one at a time and hadn't the slightest right to be greedy given the fact, as she never tired of telling me, that

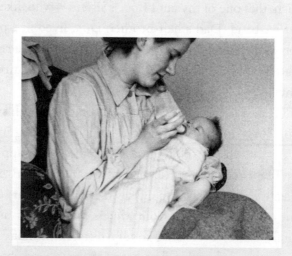

Feeding time, April 1954

both she and Dad (and particularly Dad) had often been severely famished as children.

Her reasoned appeal to my rudimentary understanding of the years before World War II—of the orphanage to which Nana Haney, reduced to destitution by her husband's death from cancer, had had to send two of my uncles and Dad, and of the shortages of food they'd known thereafter—got her nowhere despite my expanding and infernal fascination with the poverty-stricken portion of the Haney family's past.

During the week that followed Dad's announcement, time refused to fly. (I was five.)

THE ABSENCE OF DOGS from the island caused one of the two disappointments I felt on the day of the wedding. (The other was the ceremony, which bored me.) After leaving the church, Mum and Joy and Dad and I and everybody else adjourned to an enormous, run-down room distinguished by knot-niggled floorboards, naked lightbulbs, and barely whitewashed walls. This late-model cave contained, on three sides, rickety folding tables sporting glasses packed with cigarettes known as Churchman's, which, said Dad, though not frightfully posh, weren't exactly rubbish. The fourth side was home to a worm-eaten crate of an under-raised stage occupied by an upright piano, electric guitars, a trumpet, a trombone, and drums.

Two hours later and after the speeches, our ranks now distended by lots of people who hadn't been at the church, we stood in a ring, stuck out one leg and then the other, turned around, joined hands, and skipped back and forth while singing something that sounded like "Go smoky smoky"—

a redundant exhortation, since most of the celebrants, with the possible exception of the under-eights, were already smoking furiously. After that, I sat next to Mum, who often felt uncomfortable at parties, her social skills having only narrowly avoided being inoperably maimed by her none-too-loving parents.

Dad appeared to have disappeared but then, with a bottle of beer in one hand and a cigarette fizzing in the other, he reappeared—his beaklike Adam's apple and shrubbery eyebrows sticking out impressively that afternoon—followed by

Aunt Rose in 1948

a flushed-looking Rose and her bristle-headed, perspiring, lager-laden, and loudly good-humored husband.

"Here's your uncle Don," said Dad. "And your auntie Rose. You remember them, don't you?"

"Course he bloody does," yelled Don, who had not done well at school and drove double-decker buses for London Transport. "Me and Rosie made a right old fuss of 'im and Joy at the 'ospital. We all did. Sad day, that was. This is a bloody good knees-up, though. You remember me, mate, don't yer?"

"Yes," I squeaked.

"And here comes the rest of our crowd, looking a little the worse for wear and I really can't think why," said Dad, who had the physique of a grasshopper and (when especially pleased, which wasn't often) a smile as wide as a dolphin's.

UNCLE RAY AND AUNTIE EILEEN, Uncle Dick and Auntie Joan, and Uncle Dave (the oldest Haney brother) and his wife, Auntie Ena, clustered and plunged into courtesies first and, next, into banter. A few minutes later, eager to mix with less familiar members of the substrate to which, ever since the visit to the hospital, I had begun to feel I most belonged, I took a short tour of the premises.

Avoiding the dancers, I kept to the outskirts and found myself rewarded with the sight of gargantuan grannies who were trailing yards of imitation pearls and creakily cleaning the loophole backsides of a battery of naked babies while their war-painted daughters (and two generations of beer-spilling husbands) hiccupped, yapped, backslapped, and crowed among themselves. Many of the older men were clumsily coifed apparitions in ill-fitting two-piece suits, rutabaga-faced antiques with fists the size of wrecking balls, chests like damaged barrels, feet (more accustomed to work boots) rammed into well-polished second-rate shoes.

I gazed up at the unrestrained laughter and self-deprecating grins with a rapture undermined by unhappy recollections of how different this all was from my life at home, at No. 13 Mayflower Way, in Chipping Ongar (usually referred to simply as Ongar), a village in the Essex countryside, about twenty miles from London and not so far from Romford, the suburb where Dave and Ena and their daughter, Pauline, lived. Everyone seemed to know everyone here, and even

No. 13 Mayflower Way

if they didn't, they were unusually nice to you. Which was rarely the case, for as long as I lived there, in Ongar.

Dad, a grapher (that's a contraction of "telegraphist") by trade, at least appeared less serious, less harried and hounded, than usual. ("A grapher's life," he liked to say, usually when up in arms about feeling financially pinched, "is a sad one.") And Mum, who sometimes quietly, sometimes loudly, resented the fact that Dad's was little more than a steady job with modest pay and nonexistent prospects, looked oddly relaxed. She had Joy on her lap, and her curly permed hair was in just the slightest disarray from dancing, at which, unlike Dad, she was awful.

THE FOOD APPEALED TO ME as much as the bonhomie, especially the kinds that I had never tried before: the pickled onions (which Dad always bought at Christmas and which Mum, who thought them déclassé, refused to touch), the whelks (which I risked when I noticed Rose and Don eating them with the eagerness I always brought to the first-degree murder of Jelly Babies), and the prawns, whose beaded heads and slippery tails I quickly became adept at removing. Ray, a dapper man with a face like a ferret's, then taught me how to butcher winkles with a pin.

"These are quite nice," I murmured, while grappling with their slightly gamy scent.

"That's not what your mum said the first time she tried one," said Ray, who worked as a tax inspector and, to my amazement, didn't smoke. "Remember that, Eileen? First time Kitty met Mum. Over at Phillips Street. That sit-down tea we had."

"What did she say, Uncle Ray?" I asked, reminding myself that Phillips Street was in Plaistow, the part of the East End where Nana had lived both during and after the war. (Eileen and Ray still lived there, in a tiny house inherited from Eileen's mother.)

"Didn't exactly say anything," said Eileen, whose monumental bosom I'd begun to find quite a distraction. "Just pulled a face and, well, stuck to bread and butter."

"I—I like bread and butter," I bubbled.

"I do, too," she said, reapplying her lipstick, which perfectly matched the cherry-red frames of her glasses, with swift but spot-on movements of her pudgy hands. "But it's nice if you can tart it up a bit."

"I was a bit surprised," said Ray, fidgeting with the fountain pen parked in his jacket breast pocket and staring with barely disguised disgust as a rumpled Uncle Dick—who, like Dad and Uncle Dave, worked for the Commercial Cable Company—stubbed out a ready-made cigarette (Dad almost always rolled his own) in a saucer. "I mean, her father's from the flipping East End."

"That's true," said Eileen. "But her mum weren't."

"Whose mum wasn't what?" said Mum, just returned from taking care of a queasy Joy in the toilet.

"Yours, love," said Eileen. "Not from the East End."

"No, she wasn't," said Mum. Her mother, Grandma Bush, a person of refinement, had almost been disowned by her parents for marrying a penniless man who had started life as a slum kid. "But my dad is. Ray, what's John eating?"

"Winkles," said Ray.

"Winkles? Ugh!"

"Oh," said Dick. "Eating winkles, are we? Well. There you are, Kit."

"What?" said Mum.

"Your little boy's one of us," he averred, sluggishly nuzzling a welterweight glass of whiskey, the drink that eventually killed him.

"Oh, really?" said Mum, who liked the Cockneys well enough, particularly for their kindness, but had absolutely no intention of allowing her children to follow in their working-class footsteps. "What makes you so sure?"

"He looks pretty happy to me," said Dick.

" 'One of us'?" I asked, a bit belatedly.

"Yes. One of us. An East Ender—here, have a good look," said Dick, putting down his drink and, a little unsteadily, picking me up and sitting me on his shoulders.

Cigarette smoke gusted and swam before me, drifting above the cardboard suits, the slender skirts, the frill-fractured frocks, and the skyscraping updos.

Dad, who had been desperate to leave the East End and give his family a life amid breathable air and green fields, seemed less than impressed with Dick's antics but, as he always did when provoked or upset or on the verge of spiraling into vexation, held his tongue.

MY THIRD (and much looked forward to) encounter with the rest of the Haneys took place in 1960, when I was six, two Saturdays prior to Christmas. My parents had elected to host a family party for the first time. Mum's concessions to the culinary preferences of people born in the East End were cocktail

sausages on a stick, a few pickled onions, hefty ham sandwiches, mince pies (which Dad made), a couple of dozen
sausage rolls, and (at Dad's insistence) a monstrous bowl of
peanuts in the shell. These Mum considered dead common.

Almost everything else that she and Dad piled onto our
distressingly ugly Beautility dining table, whose legs resembled those of an elephant with water on the knee, seemed
more suited to a children's birthday party: cucumber sandwiches minus the crusts, fish paste sandwiches, skimpily buttered bread and cheese, and a plate of custard tartlets. A
stealthy investigation of the fridge while my parents' backs
were turned revealed, to my disappointment, that winkles,
whelks, and prawns were not on the menu.

Once reasonable justice had been done to the food,
drinking—which, by now, I had come to believe had much to
do with happiness, particularly in Don's case—came to the
fore. Dave, a withdrawn and gangly man whose clothes always seemed slightly too big for him, stuck to beer in moder-
ation because he was driving. So did Ray. Dad, who was
consistently abstemious throughout his quiet life, made a pint
of ale last all evening. Don, whose higher education as a darts
player had been undertaken in tandem with the acquisition of
an ability to easily dispose of what the English call a skinful,
put away six pints of lager. Dick, who was also driving but
didn't give what I would now refer to as a flying fuck, took
charge of a fifth (followed by another) of Johnnie Walker
Black Label, which put him in direct competition with Joy
and me for the limited ice (for orange squash) that our refrig-
erator, roughly the size of a minibar, could produce.

All of the ladies but one comported themselves sedately.
Mum had a ritual sherry for appearances' sake and then re-

verted to tea. Eileen and Ena put a moderate dent in the bottle that Mum had breached, after which they directed their attention to several boxes of chocolates. Rose sipped at a sizable glass of shandy.

Initially unnerved by the shortage of ice and the threat it represented to the routine pursuit of her favorite pastime, Joan, who worked as head cook in a factory canteen, cut up the lemons she'd had the good sense to bring, knowing, as she did, that Mum and Dad had no idea how to make a cocktail. She put the lemons in a soup bowl, wrapped it in tinfoil, and set it out on the back steps, where the lemons quickly froze solid. Shortly thereafter, they joined forces with a huge quantity of gin and a sprinkle of tonic in a tumbler (the size of a flower pot) that Joan had brought with her all the way from Rayleigh, the town in southeast Essex where she and Dick lived.

WHILE LISTENING IN on the family banter, I opened my Christmas presents. From Rose and Don, a clockwork American railway engine with a cowcatcher. From Ray and Eileen, a Bill Haley 45. From Dick and Joan, an elementary chemistry set (which Dad, quite rightly, thought I was much too young for). From Dave and Ena, a space station armed with flying saucers. I was, as always with these people, all ears and not remotely looking forward to the end of the day—not least because discipline, Mum's passion and forte, always fell back to the faraway parts of the landscape whenever my aunts and uncles were around.

"I don't half like peanuts," said Dick. "Always take me back a bit. Sitting in the cheap seats. Down the fleapit."

"What's a fleapit?" I asked.

"It's a *very* low class of cinema," said Joan. "A very low class indeed, mate. Just like the Grand in Canning Town."

"That was a right old dump," said Dad.

"It was a dump and a bloody half," said Dick. "Busted seats. Fag ends all over the place. Nobody ever swept up."

"Did it really have fleas?" I asked.

"Several million, probably," said Joan. "I used to go there when I was a girl. People came round in the intervals to spray us. Mind you, that was mainly for lice, I think."

"I thought lice lived in trenches," I said, recalling my paternal granddad's reportage of having spent hours pinching the beasts to extinction in between German bombardments.

"Been talking to poor old Harry, has he, Kit?" said Joan, her slate-gray eyes in alcoholic turmoil above the busted drawbridge of her nose.

"A bit," said Mum. "But Dad doesn't like to talk about it much."

"He was in both of them, wasn't he?" said Dick.

"Yes," said Mum. "He was. Western Front the first time round. Off to sea in the other. Me and Mum and Jackie stuck at home with an ack-ack battery just down the road, next to the PDSA. I was a nervous wreck." (Jackie was Mum's older sister.)

"What's ack-ack?" I asked, delighted that the war had now emerged as the subject of conversation among people who had experienced it.

"Antiaircraft guns," said Dick. "Want to hear a really, really big bloody bang, John? Stand next to one of those."

"Oh. I see. What's the PDSA, Mum?"

"People's Dispensary for Sick Animals, dear. Every time

those guns opened up. I couldn't help thinking. All those poor little cats and dogs. Going berserk in their cages."

"Sod the cats and dogs," said Dick, now extremely well oiled and numerous shades of vermilion. "We all went bloody berserk in our cages more than bloody once. When the Krauts came bloody well swanning up the Thames. Couldn't see a thing once they'd buggered off home. Smoke on the water. Smoke bloody everywhere. Right bunch of bastards."

"Too bloody right," said Don. "Still, you were out of it soon enough. Off to flipping India. Bit of a stroke of luck, eh?"

"Luck?" said Dick, who had spent the war as a sergeant

Dad in Cairo in 1943

instructor at a signals school in Bombay and was, though shaped like a doughnut, the snappiest-looking male at the party. "India? I sometimes think I'd rather have been shot at. Done my so-called bit somewhere else. Africa . . ."

"I doubt that," said Dave, who had fought there.

"Italy . . ."

"I don't think so," said Dad, who had somehow emerged unscathed (except for some superficial cuts) from a shell detonation that did for the two other soldiers with whom he'd taken cover in a ditch during the advance to the River Po.

At which point, Dick, refilling his glass, retreated.

THE FOURTH—and what turned out to be the last—of my childhood exposures to the congregated Haneys fell in 1962, on a Saturday in December at Don's house. (I was eight.)

At about six that morning, the sound of Dad going downstairs immediately propelled me into our kitchen, where he made me a slice of buttered toast and gently suggested that I sequester myself with a comic, preferably somewhere else, while he manufactured mince pies. Receding to the living room, I contentedly slouched on the piteous heap of ripped red moquette otherwise known as our sofa. Selecting a copy of *Victor*, I sopped up the inspirational sight of Canadian soldiers scaling Vimy Ridge with sporadic regressions for dying cries occasioned by machine guns. Next, I pored over *Lion*, the publication responsible for some of my most favored stalwarts: Squadron Leader Paddy Payne, easily reducing a luckless fleet of Mussolini's torpedo bombers to blips of blazing canvas; Robot Archie and his enterprising inventors, Ted and Ken, pioneer types who could always be relied upon to shoot

Dad in 1947

an uppity Zulu; Captain Condor, rocketing his way from one unfriendly planet to another in a quest to rid the cosmos of odious life forms. Between comics, I thought of the Haneys, almost invariably smiling, the truest of true-blue East Enders.

Two hours passed in silence and reflection broken solely by six rounds of clattering as tart tins made contact with oven racks. Dad then declared that it was time for breakfast proper and gave me a choice between Sugar Puffs and Ready Brek. Neither prospect enticed me. My request for a bacon sandwich—a delicacy that I would willingly have eaten for breakfast, dinner, and tea every day—was refused on the grounds that we would all be on "short rations" until we arrived at Don's house and began to "stuff ourselves silly." (Dinner, for those unfamiliar with a fading British vernacular, is the meal known as lunch in superior circles; breakfast is breakfast both above and below stairs; and the repast referred to as dinner by those who hunt foxes is tea to those who bet on greyhounds.)

AT TWO, THE PACE of preparations picked up. While Dad placed dozens of mince pies, layered between sheets of wax paper, in a shopping bag, Mum wrestled our shrew of an ironing board upright and, shrouded in steam, operatically slammed at the best her children's wardrobes had to offer. The creases in my worsted short trousers and the sleeves of my least inexpensive white shirt grew sharper. Joy's party skirt, a cut-price concertina of inconsistent pleats, received such a concentrated pressing that it could easily have stood up on its own.

At four o'clock we paraded in the hallway for final inspection. Mum, neatly attired in a close-fitting light gray twinset and—as usual when we went out—in heavily made-up pursuit of the illusion of respectability, straightened Dad's tie, ran a wet comb through my hair with a ferocity that still makes me flinch when I think of it, and mercilessly yanked the nut-brown straps of Joy's Start-rite shoes a notch tighter. Dad, still smarting from having been routed by Mum in an argument she'd started at lunchtime, then went out to struggle with the ignition of our embarrassingly decrepit, third-hand

Austin Seven, which had been bolted together in 1934, seemed to leak more oil than it used, and had a top speed of thirty miles per hour on the straight and level, occasionally managing a bone-shaking forty when going downhill.

Ten minutes later a very loud bang brought news of success but also extracted a burp and a gurgle from Joy, who was so prone to motion sickness that she usually decamped, with a coloring book, to the kitchen whenever I spent any time shoving my Dinky Toy die-cast model autos from one threadbare end of our echoing lounge to the other. This was not a good omen. I sat as far away as possible from her once the car was keening along Ongar High Street and periodically retching, as it always did, whenever Dad changed gear.

HAVING CROSSED THE RAIN-SLICKED sheet of iron plate that served as a bridge to a northern extreme of the Isle of Dogs—where some of the damage inflicted by German bombers had yet to be undone—we juddered down street after street of uniform two-story row houses with three stooped windows and a door that opened directly onto the pavement. It was about six o'clock when we arrived at Don's house. In the weeks leading up to the party, I had come to think of No. 43 Harbinger Road as my personal promised land, the place, above all others, where I could be free of domestic discord—and of being smacked by Mum whether or not I'd done anything to deserve it.

Weighted with presents and pies, we invaded without knocking, tripped along two feet of hallway, and stepped down into the postage-stamp living room, where the rest of "all of us," as well as a horde of Don's neighbors, were conspicuously in the kind of good mood that Mum and Dad could rarely match. Don gave me a grin and an almost obscenely dramatic thumbs-up the instant he saw me. He was smartly dressed in navy blue V-neck, white nylon shirt, funereal tie, sober gray trousers, and shiny black shoes. From behind a bar he'd somehow squeezed between the sofa and the telly, he was dispensing—with a brisk efficiency that I imagined surely had something to do with his magical ability to drive an enormous bus—beer, stout, lager, Bristol Cream Sherry, Stone's Green Ginger Wine, Sandeman Port, Gordon's Gin, and Black Label.

We pushed our way through to the kitchen, where a young woman who turned out to be one of Rose's sisters was regaling the children with hugs, kisses, tissues when needed, directions to the lavatory, and paper cups of Robinson's Orange Squash ("dilute to taste"), Ribena ("the blackcurrant health drink"), Whiteway's Cydrax (which was nonalcoholic and came in a tin), and White's Cream Soda. Rose herself, glamorous and immaculate in gray pencil skirt and pastel blouse, was busy trying to fix a four-year-old's nosebleed. I asked her sister for a cold sausage sandwich and turned to the table, which was buried under the kind of food I'd last seen in all its glory at the wedding, three years before.

Blank-faced pickled onions were drowning in vinegar. Skewered at the midriff, squadrons of cocktail sausages were lined up like fatalities on stretchers. Bulking wedges of Cheddar sat at the back in the shadows of sandwiched ham, triangulations of pork and quashed bread that were shedding meltdown butter and a hint of the sty. Packets of dates, lids tidily tilted, sang discreetly of the Levant to winkles, whelks, and prawns. Thick-sliced bread surrounded an enormous teapot capable of accommodating the Mad Hatter and every last one of his friends. I was, once again, in my element, in a mystical place where life reached its cheerfully uproarious zenith.

A FEW MINUTES LATER, my favorite people from Romford descended.

"Hello, John," said Ena. Her Cockney accent had a queenly edge. She knew the East End inside out but, as Dad put it, did not belong to the "effing-and-blinding brigade." She was, I think, an example of the stillness at the heart of the Cockney typhoon, of the silence that sweeps through the ranks when the last dud cracker has been ripped, the paper hats casually flicked into the fireplace, and the gas meter glutted with Boxing Day's last shilling. It's a soundlessness that greets me these days when an atavistic whim lures me into seedy pubs east of London Bridge, places where time stopped several decades ago.

"Hello, Auntie Ena."

"Fed up with the flying saucers yet? Lost them all by now?"

"No."

"Good. Something tells me you're going to like what we're giving you this year. I told Dave it was his turn to go down the shops and get things sorted."

"Bet he didn't like that. Dad hates going shopping."

"Oh, I don't know about that, dear. He bought himself a new fishing rod while he was at it."

"Another one? He's already got loads."

"It's called a hobby, John. And we all know what yours is."

"Do you?"

"Yes, we do. Reading—does that ring a bell?"

"That's not a hobby."

"I think it might be. Costs your mum and dad a bob or two. I took a peek at your bedroom last time we was over. Right little library. Not just Noddy books and *Beano* annuals, either. Quality stuff. Quite the brainy one, aren't yer?"

"I'm not brainy—I'm rotten at sums," I demurred. Indeed, I'd spent hours standing in the corner for my arithmetical ineptitude.

"So was I. Still, can't be good at everything, can you, Dave?"

Dave, who had been captured by the Germans and spent four years in prison camps in Italy, Czechoslovakia, and Poland, said nothing and handed me an envelope.

"But you already sent us a Christmas card."

"It's a bit more fun than a Christmas card," said Ena.

"I know what it is," said Pauline. "Shall I tell you?"

"Shush, Pauline," said Dave. "It's supposed to be a surprise."

The envelope contained a card with a piece of paper pasted into it that reminded me of money and bore the legend "10/-."

My confusion immediately deepened.

"It's a book token."

"A what?"

"A book token. You take it into a bookshop, pick out ten

bob's worth of books, give them the token, and the books are all yours."

I liked the sound of that.

"LA BAMBA" MUST have been played a hundred times before the party wound down. Once the neighbors were gone, the remnants of the party settled in the living room, and Aunt Rose put the kettle on for a final pot of tea.

Dick was scarlet, as was Joan. Ray was burrowing his way through a packet of crisps. Eileen and Ena and cousin Pauline were gobbling the last of the chocolates. Dad, having stubbed out the last of his Woodbines (a dirt-cheap brand of ready-mades he smoked on special occasions), was back on the Golden Virginia, his loose tobacco of choice. Mum, who hardly ever smoked but tended to go for a better class of cigarette when she did, was savoring a Piccadilly cadged from Dick. Don was slumped next to me on the sofa, a packet of Embassy and a lighter lodged in his lap, and seemed to have fallen asleep. In fact, however, he was wide awake and, as Dad would have said, "compos mentis," as he proved when the tea arrived.

"Well, Denis," he said, fishing five cubes of sugar from the bowl and winking at me with a look that suggested, to my delight, that a cat of some kind would soon be among the pigeons, "you've got a right old drive home in front of you. Especially after a do like this. What made yer move all the flipping way out to Ongar? Yer a London boy, Den. Same goes for you, Dick."

Dick kept quiet.

"What about Dave?" Dad countered, extinguishing a half-smoked roll-your-own and—this was a strictly working-class feat at which I always marveled—tucking it behind his ear. "He's all the way out in Romford."

"I know that," said Don. "But Romford's not the country, is it? I mean. It's a bit of a walk from Dave's house to the nearest bloody field."

"Might just as well be in London," said Ena. "When I'm out shopping in Romford Market, there's Cockneys all over the place." (Thousands of Cockneys had moved to Romford in the decade that followed the war.)

"Actually, it was my idea," said Mum, in a steely tone.

"Really?" said Rose.

"Yes," said Mum, reaching across the coffee table with a spat-upon hankie wound around a finger to remove a smear of sausage fat from my chin. "It was. When me and Den were living in Rainham. Which I didn't like a bit to begin with. Just after John was born. I was out for a walk. I had John in the pram and I saw some kids fighting and swearing. I couldn't believe the filthy things they were saying. It was absolutely revolting. And when Denis got home that night, I told him. I said: 'We can't stay here. John's not growing up like those kids. I just won't bloody well stand for it. We've got to move.' So we did. I put a deposit on our house in Ongar—best five quid *I* ever spent—about a week later. I think we're getting our money's worth. John's doing quite well—except for his sums—at school."

She delivered this speech with a visible measure of pride from which I took comfort despite the fact that she could be alarmingly pushy when apprising me, as she often did until I was in my late teens—at which point she sensibly threw in the towel—of the importance of doing one's best.

"Were they swearing *that* badly?" said Don.

"Yes," sniffed Mum. "They were."

"I can see Kit's point," said Dick. "Where are those poor bloody kids going to be fifteen years from now? Earning next to bloody nothing and spending it down the pub. Bet you I'm right. And I know it's unfair. But a bit of bloody polish and some decent flaming diction don't half come in handy at times."

"You're right there," said Dave. "They certainly banged the diction into us at the orphanage. Remember those elocution classes, Den?"

"How could I forget?" replied Dad.

"Well," said Don, "me and Rosie are going to 'ave kids and I'm blowed if I'm moving. I like it 'ere. And you'll never catch my nippers swearing."

"Hmmph," said Eileen. "I wouldn't be too flipping sure about that. Boys will be boys, you know. Still, you might have girls. It's probably easier with girls."

"Probably," said Don. "I flaming well 'ope so. Besides, swearing isn't ladylike."

"Mum didn't half swear," said Dick.

"That's different," said Ray. "Mum only swore when she'd been provoked. And she got provoked a lot."

"True enough," said Dave. "What with the dog's life she had to lead."

This immediately reminded me of the fistfight Nana had apparently had (over the lease to a rented house) with one of her sisters in 1934. As a result she'd been bound over, in a magistrate's court in a part of east London called Stratford, to keep the peace for a year.

"I provoked her once, you know," said Dad.

"Just the once? Come off it," Dave replied.

"I mean really provoked her. And I wasn't expecting it, either. First time I bought a house."

"You what?" said Don.

"First time I bought a house. She hit the roof. There I was. Slaving over the paperwork. Me and Kitty were living at Mum's, remember? Right after we got married. And in she comes one Saturday morning and says. 'Denis,' she says. 'I can't believe you're buying a house. Know what you are? A traitor to the working class.' Really upset me."

"I didn't get it in the neck like that," said Don.

"Me neither," said Dick, followed by Dave and Ray.

"Oh, well," said Dad. "I can only suppose she got used to it."

"Mum never minced her words," said Ray. "Remember that really bad afternoon, Den? Daylight raid. September 1940. Windows blown out. Front door gone. Half the roof off. And what does she say? 'I'm not moving for that bastard Hitler. They'll have to carry me out.' "

At this, overwhelmed by a joyousness, bound up with a love of irreverence that I had now come to associate exclusively with the Cockneys, I laughed so hard that the tea in my mouth exited my nose and hit Joy squarely in the face.

IT WAS PROBABLY well past midnight when we left. I was feeling buoyantly bloated. Dad was sober. Mum looked tired. And Joy, rinsed of tea stains, was fast asleep. Everyone came

With Mum and Dad, 1954

out to see us off, and as the Austin pulled away, I knelt on the backseat and waved till a jolt to the left expunged aunts, uncles, cousin from sight. Dad retrieved a half-smoked cigarette from the Austin's grubby ashtray and lit it.

I found myself thinking of Christmas Eve and Christmas Day, to be spent that year beneath the roof of No. 207 Woodford Avenue, the cavernous three-bedroom semidetached in Redbridge owned by my maternal grandfather, Harry Augustus Bush. Then I cracked a stray peanut and immediately dreamed of the Cockneys—and realized that my fourth exposure to people from London's East End had persuaded me that I actually wanted to move there.

I cherished the sheer exultation I felt in my Cockney kin's presence, a sense of rapture I'd have been astonished to learn I was not to revisit until forty-four years later, at a watering hole in a hard-hearted town a much-contested ocean and a legendary suspension bridge away.

I would also have been appalled to discover that I was only to see the Haney mob entire again twice in my life, at two weddings with nothing in common but the fact that, at both of them, Joan got hopelessly smashed. Pauline's wedding proved a happy occasion; Joy's did not.

CHAPTER 2

Kippers and Custard

. . . .

THE WEEKLY EXPEDITIONS TO GRANDPA'S WERE USUALLY UN-
dertaken by Mum and Joy and me. To my disappointment, we
were only rarely joined by Dad, for he was in constant pursuit
of overtime.

For Mum, the first stage of the journey involved firmly
screwing her fidgeting offspring into their shoes and then
briskly pegging them into mildly militaristic gabardine raincoats. Next, she would juggle Joy into her reins, and we
would then walk to Ongar Station, which, when Joy and I
were small, was served by a steam locomotive.

If we arrived with time to spare, I would jettison Joy and
Mum, dementedly scuttle to the far end of the platform, and
beg to be allowed up onto the footplate by the driver and his
assistant so as to get a glimpse of the mechanism's guts, the
heap of snarling coals whose energy would soon remove us, if
only for a fistful of hours, from the setting of the tensions—

With Mum and Grandpa and Grandma Bush, 1954

which I didn't, at that time, quite understand—that had already begun to degrade relations between my parents.

Having seated us in good order, Mum would reach into her shopping bag for fail-safe antidotes to tedium: a midget bar of chocolate for each of us and, for my eyes only, a copy of *Knockout*, a comic with whose risible aid she was, with a determination that frequently sparked my hidden annoyance, teaching me how to read.

The train would trundle southwestward, its boxy Edwardian carriages swaying from side to side. I would do my best to read the speech balloons aloud to Mum, paying attention when precisely corrected and reveling, when not corrected, in the escapades of Buster, *Knockout*'s leading ne'er-do-well, who, I would eventually discover, went by the name of Tracassin in the land of *beurre noisette*.

THE WORDPLAY that marked these excursions also included the visions evoked by the names of the stations we passed through and by those of other stops on the Underground, all absorbed one word at a time as I picked my way across a map of the system.

The suggestion of grandeur in "Blake Hall," the name of the first westbound stop on the line, was later confirmed by knowledge of the seventeenth-century English admiral whose weevil-eating tars sent so many Dutchmen to a watery mausoleum that stretched from the North Sea to Trinidad. (To my embarrassment, my boyish admiration for that officer, Robert Blake, seems to have persisted.)

The second element of the name of the next stop, North Weald, a village immortalized in the annals of the Battle of Britain as a frequently battered but never bowed aerie of Hurricanes and Spitfires, vaguely echoed the "even keel" to whose importance in ships of state and vessels like his dinghy of a house Dad sometimes referred in rare moments of waxing political.

Rhyming with "stepping" and sitting in the middle of a forest was Epping, where Mum—umbrella drawn and pushchair at the ready for whenever Joy chose to grow weary of trotting—would goad us across a footbridge to catch the electric train that would take us almost the rest of the way. Sometimes, in a bustle to board as the doors were about to close, we would stumble into a smoking carriage, its floor half-encrusted with spent cigarettes and spackled with more ash than Etna.

THE FINAL INSTALLMENT of our journey to Grandpa's house began at South Woodford, where, if I was in luck, Mum would come to a halt at the fish shop next to the station to buy something for tea, leaving me ghoulishly free to gaze at a bucket of eels, creatures Mum never bought. I was mesmerized by their sleekness, seduced by the circling of their snouts and streaming tails, and I always hoped, with all my heart, to see one hacked to bits before we left. Only at the midpoint of my spotted youth would Mum share with me the not quite improbable story that I promptly dubbed the eel joke. She had been shopping for haddock with Nana Haney in one of the East End's least lovely (which is going some) open-air markets when an eel slipped free of a fishmonger's fingers and came to wriggly rest in the lingerie stand next door, atop an undergarment plainly designed for frenzied removal. "That's the longest bleedin' thing those knickers are going to see," declared Nana.

A trolleybus would carry us all the way through pancake-flat Gants Hill to the intersection of Woodford Avenue and Beehive Lane, where the vehicle stopped a hundred yards from Grandpa's house. His circumstances, though undeniably modest, were a definite improvement on the poverty into which he had been born, on February 15, 1892, in Limehouse, which Mum had grimly described to me as, at that time, "absolutely the very worst slum in London."

GRANDPA'S FATHER, Michael Doyle, a docker of Irish and Catholic ancestry, spent almost every penny he earned on beer. This left the family sometimes dependent on his barely literate wife, Maria, a frequently unemployed seamstress. In the Doyles' half a basement, the luxuries—meaning soap, coal, cooking oil, and sugar—were not so much in short supply as virtually unknown. The most consequential necessity was procured not by parting with cash but by dint of child labor deployed at nightfall.

Every evening when the street markets closed, Grandpa scoured the gutters for anything remotely edible discarded by bakers and grocers—mildewed greens, wrinkled oranges, waspish apples, scabby mangolds, aging bread. The calls of nature brought on by this diet of worms were answered, as they had been for centuries in the more overcrowded parts of the metropolis, at a public privy that often overflowed in the rain.

Grandpa's education, at a time when elementary learning was theoretically compulsory, was intermittent at best, and, according to Mum, his knowledge of the language as written and read might well have remained inchoate but for the kindness of a certain Mr. Hardiman, a clerk (who, one suspects, had missed his vocation) at the Limehouse Public Library, to which a ragamuffin Grandpa had paid his first visit solely in order to keep warm. Mr. Hardiman somehow contrived to inject Grandpa with the sufficiency of knowledge that eventually made him an inveterate scribbler of sensitive love letters and a dyed-in-the-wool subscriber to *Reader's Digest*.

By the time World War I (which came to be known as the Great War) broke out, Grandpa had not only added singing and dancing to his accomplishments but was also, Mum surmised, beginning to feel more and more that his life to date—his very identity—was something he wanted no part of. And that, she imagined, was why, in November 1915, he renounced his Catholicism, changed his name to Bush (his mother's maiden name), and enlisted in the regiment known as the City of London Yeomanry.

He gave his occupation as "music hall artist," but he never performed professionally again, confining his demonstrations to a minute or two of tapping and warbling for the occasional entertainment of his daughters and, in later years, his grandchildren, both of whom worshipped him and, now and then, whenever he had what I came to call the hard look in his eyes—haunted, remote, and forbidding—found him a little scary.

THE HUNDRED-YARD DASH to the portals of Grandpa's house was a race I always won. Ratting and tatting produced Auntie Jackie, and while she and Mum prized Joy from her pushchair, I would run racketing down the hallway, which reeked of embrocation and Wright's Coal Tar Soap, toward the light that was leaching from the half-closed kitchen door. This sprint brought with it the stink of cigar smoke (a stench I still savor), the bittersweet scent of Caribbean rum, the on-cue clank of a kettle being positioned over a burner, and the cheering and jeering of the televised sports in which Grandpa was always engrossed on Saturday afternoons.

—

FROM THE TIME I was four until I turned fourteen, No. 207 Woodford Avenue was my home away from home, a house where much was eaten and, as I was only to realize much later, surprisingly little said. This was the house where Mum had grown up and where I'd first heard of Narvik, Limehouse, Ypres, and the Somme, whose names, with every telling, grew a little more redolent of an infinite and hidden despair.

My maternal grandmother, Katherine Bush, née Isdale, was a sturdy woman of dignified bearing whose skirt, blouse, and apron were always as starched as a pillowcase pressed by a Lascar. As I burst in, she'd blow out the match she had used to light the gas, drop it into Grandpa's ashtray, an irregular chunk of myopic glass, and bend down to give me a perfumed peck on the cheek. (Grandpa and Grandma had met during World War I and emigrated to the United States in 1920; they had been forced to return to England because Grandma could no longer stand the heat of summers in Pennsylvania and had been warned by her doctor, in 1928, that she would die if she dared to stay another year.)

Enthroned three feet from the television in his favorite chair, a pawnbroker's antiquarian whose fiddlestick arms, rattail upholstery, and ineffective springs he loved obsessively, Grandpa would, from my point of view, be visible on the horizon of the vast expanse of oilskin covering the kitchen table as a perfectly still shock of silver hair emitting a steam bath of smoke. In the American accent that had marked his every utterance for the past thirty years, he would bark "Hi, Jaaaaahn!" while keeping his gunmetal eyes trained on big-bellied wrestlers tying each other in knots.

With Grandpa in the back garden at
No. 207 Woodford Avenue, 1957

I would pull up a stool next to Grandpa and cradle the first
of several mugs of Grandma's tea, which was not only tooth-
dissolving but also necessitated unnumbered trips to the outhouse, a cobwebbed cupboard smelling of disinfectant and
thoughtlessly equipped with a brand of far from absorbent

toilet paper whose utilization without revulsion required a degree of dexterity. (The outhouse was, however, as I often reminded myself, a definite improvement on the conditions wherein Grandpa had relieved himself as a boy.)

Every now and then, a jam tart or a chocolate cupcake came with the tea. On less extravagant afternoons, I made do with a handful of sweets. Time would then pass until half-light and a kind of bliss I seem to miss increasingly as I grow older. On my favorite nights, the overdose of ecstasy was fully explained by bangers. Once the sausages had been punctured and thus dispossessed of all inclination to spatter when seared, Grandma transferred them in squealing batches to an immensely wide fry pan, there to squirm and smoke until a crescendo of sizzling proclaimed them done.

As soon as she'd scooped them onto our plates, we would hack away while they were still almost too hot to eat, still shimmering with lard. The savory brown sauce we used as a condiment would creep across the bone-white china like an oil spill, slowly swiping the gelatinous smile from the faces of the nearby fried eggs. Then we'd mop it all up with doorsteps, super-thick slices of buttered white bread. And then more doorsteps, this time painted with Marmite, an incredibly salty, yeast-based spread that is guaranteed to horrify anyone who didn't acquire a taste for it within a couple of years of leaving the womb.

The staring eyes and sunken cheeks of non-banger nights belonged to mackerel, whitebait, skate, kippers, plaice, haddock, and herring, slapped with butter and sprinkled with salt to taste. The whitebait was either grilled to the consistency of a cracker or shallow-fried without flour (seasoned or otherwise) in one or two weighty batches, thus producing the clumping effect so forcefully decried by Jane Grigson. Her stipulation of brown bread (buttered) and a litter of lemon quarters as the ideal accompaniment would undoubtedly have been viewed with skepticism by Grandpa had he lived long enough to have been in a position to supplement his personal library (an idiosyncratic mix of seed catalogues, pocket encyclopedias, Agatha Christie, Mickey Spillane, Dana's *Two Years Before the Mast*, Conrad's *Lord Jim*, and *The Call of the Wild*) with a copy of *English Food*.

SO GRANDMA'S TABLE was limited but not quite as dramatically circumscribed as it had been three decades earlier, when she and Grandpa (and their daughters, Betty and Jackie, both

With Joy, 1958

of whom had been born in the United States) arrived back in England and took up residence in a single room at No. 207.

Katherine's mother had bought the house with the few hundred pounds that had, Mum said, survived the embezzlement of most of the Isdale family fortune (they had, I'd also been told, at one time owned land in Scotland). It was now inhabited not only by Grandma's parents but also by a semi-transient gaggle of other relatives who were, financially speaking, on what Dad would have called their beam ends. Mum's accounts of the indignities of living with so many people in such impossibly close quarters saddened me decisively and, I sometimes feel, beyond repair when I first heard them. They also began to make me persistently suspicious of all manifestations of happiness, including my own.

In late October 1929, Wall Street crashed. Mum was born ten weeks later. Grandpa, who had made only a precarious living as a butcher in America and since returning to England, now lost his job and began to look for any kind of employment he could get. The quest quickly took him back to a part of the world he hated: the London docks. Six days a week for the next six years, Grandpa walked ten miles to the docks and ten miles back. In a good week, he found work on three days, and what he earned from humping sacks of coal and sugar, when combined with my grandmother's careful dips into her savings, barely sufficed to keep five mouths properly fed.

IN 1935, the Bush family's fortunes began to look up, but only a bit. Grandpa landed a job as a steward with a shipping line and spent a fair portion of the next four years on the transatlantic route, working on the first *Queen Mary* and, later, on

the *Majestic*. Having grown more and more adept at carrying
eight plates of expensive food from kitchen to first class without so much as a falter, in the summer of 1939 he was promoted to senior steward and transferred to the *Georgic*. She
was one of the many liners eventually commandeered as
troopships during World War II. Grandpa was nearly mute
on the subject of the first of his world wars, but more willing
to tell a tin-hat story or four about his life on the ocean grave
during the years that intervened between the German con-
quest of Norway and the raising of the hammer and sickle
above the Reichstag.

In 1940 the *Georgic* took part in the evacuation of British
troops from Narvik—"The decks were awash with blood
that day," Grandpa once remarked, a half-smoked cigar in
one horny paw, a cucumber sandwich (crust attached) in the
other. This casual reference to gallons of gore both revolted
and entranced me. Later, she assisted in the evacuation of
British and Allied soldiers from Brest and St. Nazaire, where
she was repeatedly assaulted, without success, from the air.
Her luck ran out, but only temporarily, in 1941, when, while
anchored off Port Tewfik, in Egypt, she was attacked by Axis
planes: her fuel oil caught fire, and the hundreds of tons of
ammunition she was carrying started to explode.

The ship began to list in a matter of seconds, and most of
the crew (including Grandpa, who didn't know how to swim)
sensibly hurled themselves over the side, as too did the human
component of her cargo—eight hundred Italian internees
who were, said Grandpa, pretty damned upset about the watery pickle in which their fellow Fascists had landed them.
Grandpa's own departure from the burning deck was less
than dignified because the enemy had caught him not just

napping, as he put it, but with a whole lot more than his pants down. And that was how Grandpa fell into the warm embrace of the Gulf of Suez wearing nothing but his boots and a helmet.

Salvaged three months later and towed to Karachi and then to Bombay for repairs, the *Georgic* continued to serve as a troopship for the rest of the war. In June 1945, Grandpa came home on leave just in time to cast his vote for the Labour Party, campaigning at that crucial point in its history on a platform of "Fair Shares for All" and led by a privately educated former Army officer and veteran of the Gallipoli campaign named Clement Attlee.

According to Mum, on July 26, when the results were declared (Labour had won by a landslide), Grandpa and Grandma, who were sitting in the kitchen at No. 207 with bread and beef dripping and a one-egg sponge on the table and the radio blaring, raided the drinks cabinet. Grinning from one ear to another, Grandpa carefully poured four glasses of sherry (two were for Mum and Jackie), inverted his own, said something unrepeatable about Winston Churchill, and sang the Popeye song.

THE MOST UNPLEASANT details of Grandpa's life in the Great War revealed themselves slowly.

"Kippers and custard," Grandpa once crowed—shortly after Grandma had been diagnosed with cancer—as we whiled away a sodden afternoon inventing unlikely meals. My suggestion, rice pudding and raw onions, had provoked a chorus of nauseated growls. Mum's appeal to semolina and gravy came in a close second. Jackie's proposition of chocolate-coated carrots, a delicacy worthy of the molecular gastronomists who have recently taken the ridiculous mainstream in San Sebastián and Barcelona, also garnered a chattering of applause. But Grandpa had thrashed us all. "Kippers and custard," he said yet again, with a grimace.

Conceding defeat, I ripped open my third packet of Jelly Babies, tipped them out onto a doily, sorted them by color, and, as I still do, scoffed the pink ones first. I then resumed my tea-swilling scrutiny of the comical misfortunes of a slavishly deferential, severely incompetent soldier named Corporal Clott. At which point Dad piped up, noting that he had once seen some singularly evil prisoners (Azerbaijani Muslims of the Turkestan Division of the Wehrmacht, he believed, who had, he said, apparently delighted in the indiscriminate killing of civilians) feasting on bully beef, plum pudding, and tea all cooked up together in a stockpot the size of a tank.

A few minutes later, Grandpa, much to the surprise of the adults in the room and much to the delight of the seven-year-old jingo sitting next to him, chimed in with a war-related memory of the culinary indignities sometimes heaped on soldiers in the middle of a fight.

THE INCIDENT, possibly apocryphal, took place on a rainy day in December 1916. Somewhere near Arras, a dog-tired Grandpa and a handful of his equally exhausted colleagues (dismounted cavalry at this point) in a company of the Suffolk Regiment, to which he'd been transferred, were detailed to guard some prisoners. One of these, when dinnertime—cold potatoes—came around, found himself at something of a disadvantage because his jaw had been badly dislocated by a blow, Grandpa guessed, from a rifle butt.

One of the German NCOs (noncommissioned officers), to the extreme fascination of friend and foe alike, promptly took the bull of disfigurement by its procrustean horns, quickly transforming a spittle of spud and a little cold tea into a stodge that he then gently spoon-fed, a splotch at a time, into the injured soldier's mouth to enable him to swallow it.

Everything went quiet. I thought of a grown-up man— a soldier—being fed like a baby and felt a prickling of unease. Mum had turned away and was staring, tight-jawed, out the window.

I deflected my attention to a packet of Smith's Crisps, carefully breaking the cellophane and the silence and nimbly extracting the twist of blue paper that held the salt. Jackie deposited another cup of tea at my elbow. Joy chewed her green Jelly Babies (which I didn't like), unprotesting. Grandpa turned the television on. Dad disinterestedly forged himself yet another anorexic roll-up. My mouth was full of salt-flat slime. Jackie stuffed plates in the oven. Mum unwrapped sausages. Thus was the happiness I knew at Grandpa's a little tinged with horror. It continued, as always, to rain.

THE ONLY LENGTHY account of Grandpa's travails in the Great War that I heard from Grandpa himself (rather than from Mum) took root in my memory on a Sunday afternoon in 1962, when I was eight. Grandma had been dead for three years.

Dad had dropped us off in Redbridge the previous morning, and Mum and Joy and I had spent the night in the bed-

room that she and Jackie and Grandma and Grandpa and
Betty had shared in the 1930s. Breakfast—ham and eggs—
was a hushed affair for the simple reason that the Ongar contingent were still half-asleep, having been kept awake all night
by the traffic on Woodford Avenue.

The rest of the morning was even quieter. Jackie (who had
an upset stomach) and Joy (who had an earache) took a long nap,
while Mum trekked off to the nearest Nonconformist church.
Grandpa, who never went to church—and refused to have a
Bible in the house because, as he once told Mum, his experiences
in the Great War had persuaded him that the redemption of hu-
manity would be a travesty of justice—strode off to the pub. I
stayed home with a pile of comics and the onset of a cold.

By twelve o'clock, the silence had grown oppressive. So I
tiptoed into the sitting room and stared at the photographs,
many of which were yellowed, black-and-white, spider-
veined, sepia, mouse-chewed.

GRANDMA, YOUNG, in floppy hat and flowing dress, a daydream on a steamer (or maybe a yacht) on the Danube. Mum
and Jackie, as teenagers, with Betty, who died in Toronto of
tuberculosis and lung cancer not long after I was born. Betty's
twin children, Danny and Diane, barely smiling, caught just
before their disappearance into the mysteries of fostering and
adoption. (Their father had died of cirrhosis of the liver in
1947.) Grandma's brother, Jim, shipmaster, fierce, ferrous
beard, telescope, peaked cap, impregnable trousers, and
braid. Jim's only son, Simon, who died in a Japanese prison
camp in Burma. Grandpa, in the Great War, with Dora, the
last of the horses he rode. There were, of course, no pictures

Jackie and Mum with their older sister,
Betty, and Betty's son, Danny, 1943

of Grandpa as a boy, the family having been far too poor for
photography, just as there were, in our house, no pictures of
Dad that predated his days in the Army.

AT ONE O'CLOCK the house came back to life. Mum returned
from church and Jackie began preparing an unusually rudimentary dinner, fish fingers with instant potato and frozen
peas, followed by leftover trifle. At half past two, Grandpa,
stinking of cigars and existentialism, returned home to discover that Jackie had given me his fish fingers and that he
would have to make do with dessert.

Armed with a teaspoon and a bowl of a substance once
dismissed by Grigson as a "mean travesty made with yellow,
packaged sponge cakes, poor sherry, and powdered custards,"
he retreated to his armchair, where he toyed with his food for

a minute and then fell asleep. A couple of hours later, Jackie gave him a gentle prod and a mug of tea and turned on the television. Which was when I assailed him with an impossibly broad question inspired by my recent reading of a story about the Great War in a comic called *Valiant*.

"What was it really like in the trenches, Grandpa?"

Mum, who was spreading butter on half a dozen doorsteps while keeping an eye on the sausages for Jackie, who still wasn't feeling well and had gone upstairs to the indoor lavatory rather than cope with the outhouse, let out a short sigh.

"I just wondered, that's all, Mum."

"I know, dear."

"Well, Johnny O'Haney," purred Grandpa, "where would you like me to begin?"

"How about the middle?" I quipped.

"Don't be flippant, John," said Mum. "There's nothing funny about war, you know. There was nothing funny about that war—or the last one. And the next one will be even worse."

At that point, Joy, who had been somewhat traumatized the previous week when a jet taking part in the North Weald Air Show had screamed over Ongar low enough to leave us all feeling quite stunned, burst into tears.

IN THE HEAVILY contested fissures and other unsafe billets where he and his mates in the 2nd Battalion of the Suffolk Regiment, along with hundreds and thousands of other unfortunates, fought and died, warm days in general and dog days in particular were a double-edged sword.

The remains of many a comrade and acquaintance, attended by rats as fat (he said) as my rabbit, Thumper, lay all too often a stone's throw away from the land of the sunburned living and displayed every stage of decomposition from limited (relatively well preserved) to moderate (barely recognizable) to advanced (flyblown heaps of tattered khaki, splintered cartilage, creeping sequestra, and wisps of wayward flesh).

Bad weather, though, brought discomforts all its own. Corpses froze; their faces quickly sank through shades of gray to lustrous blue to the mirror-bright sheen of some rotten figs he had once seen children squabbling over next to an open sewer in Alexandria. When it rained, as it did for weeks on end, the survivors stood waist deep in water at times with their rifles held above their heads, biting hard on nothing when the agony of trench foot became almost intolerable and chewing on bully beef and munching on biscuits when fragmentation shells wiped out the ration party.

One morning in Lent Grandpa was back on Dora, fairly close to the Hindenburg Line. The blast from the shell that struck the frozen mud in front of his horse slammed her skyward, smashed her front legs, and tore a hole in her belly. Grandpa was thrown from the saddle and came to winded rest in her intestines. (He always spoke of Dora tenderly and sometimes permitted my sister and me to finger the scars on his forearms and wrists, minuscule blisters that barely concealed the slivers of shrapnel and fragments of fieldstone he'd been carrying inside him since Dora's extinction.)

"AND THAT WAS the end of that for you," said Jackie. "I'm surprised at you, Daddy. Isn't John a bit young for this sort of thing?"

"No," said Mum, a bit metallically. "I don't think he is. I don't think the truth ever hurts."

"Oh, doesn't it?" said Jackie, beating a tip-tap path to the oven in her stilettos and sounding rather cross. "Let's ask John what he thinks."

Grandpa, his left hand clutching the table as his right lost its grip on the length of an imaginary lance, seemed confused. He gaped at Jackie and then at Mum and then at Dad, who had just walked in, and finally at me.

With Joy in the back garden at
No. 207 Woodford Avenue, 1957

"But," I stuttered. "But. But. Grandpa and his friends—were very brave. Weren't they?"

"Yes, they were," sang the old soldier's daughters.

Grandpa, almost hysterically, begged to differ.

"Ha!" he hooted, brandishing *The Cruel Sea,* another of the handful of novels he always had his nose in—or so it seemed to me—when he wasn't swigging fifths of rum, trouncing Jackie at draughts (he called it "checkers"), scoffing fat sausages, staring at the TV, or, in the fug of a wretched pub on Beehive Lane, holding court amid his fellow atheists. "If I ever get to the bottom of 'brave,' you'll be the first to know. You want to know about 'brave,' Johnny boy? Learn about the Russians. They showed the Germans a thing or two."

Even Dad, who wasn't the socialist he later became and rarely agreed with anything his father-in-law, whom he cordially detested, had to say, concurred. "Your granddad's right," he said, polishing (and scratching) his glasses with a hankie in need of a wash. "I'll tell you a bit about it when you're older."

"Why not now?" I entreated.

"Because it's teatime, silly. Do you want a sausage or don't you?"

CHAPTER 3

Bottomless Bumpers of Port

. . . .

EARLY IN THE SUMMER OF 1959, SHORTLY AFTER GRANDMA
Bush died, Jackie suggested (and Mum concurred) that it
would do us good to loosen the mourning bands and take a
proper holiday. We went to the Hillcrest Dene, the necessarily respectable hotel in Bournemouth—on the English
Riviera—where, I later learned, my parents had previously
been reduced, not once but twice, to perplexity and embarrassment by their ignorance of upper-middle-class foods.

On the first occasion, which fell in the course of a long
weekend in 1949 and followed a typical Phillips Street Friday
of shellfish at five and gambling for matchsticks at dusk, Mum
and Dad, newly engaged, sat down to lunch in the Hillcrest
Dene's cathedral of a dining room and found themselves confronted with a slender wedge whose tangerine flesh reminded
them of an orange-flavored Popsicle. Its accompaniment appealed even less, resembling, as it did, Mum felt, a streak of
face powder. (It was actually ground ginger.)

Dad, I learned later, thought hard for a moment that turned into minutes, fiddling with his napkin ring as the enigma began to perspire. Illumination finally flamed in the form of a distant memory. The hotel fizzled and flopped before his eyes, taking with it Mum's imploring visage and every ounce of barely affordable sunlight. In its stead rose a rippling glimpse of ten tiny boys, little fish out of water, sitting circa 1935 in the clamorous kitchen of a grand hotel and eating a minor reprise of the interminable dinner they had earlier served to the patrons of the Alexandra Orphanage, brilliantined captains of finance and industry with diamond-studded wives in sumptuous tow. A split-second later, the Hillcrest Dene flashed back into view and Dad announced that, on the basis of his severely limited experience of seven-course dining complete with a cliff face of Stilton and bottomless bumpers of port, the orange stuff was probably some kind of melon.

Mum, who was nineteen at the time, continued to cringe while fingering the slightly floppy collar of her dress, the first one she'd been allowed to buy with no supervision from Grandma. A total stranger to the empiricism that was one of Dad's multiple strong points, she finally assaulted her portion with the force of false confidence and duly sent it spinning across the room.

The young couple's second encounter with an unfamiliar appetizer took place a year later, at six o'clock in the evening on the second night of their honeymoon, and resulted, courtesy of Mum's attempt to carry the day with the aid of a teaspoon and sugar tongs, in the deposit of something resembling a hairball on the promenade deck of a tea trolley. Neither of them ever touched an artichoke again.

Mum in 1949

SINCE JOY AND I had never been on a holiday of any kind before, Mum's announcement that we were going on one produced considerable bafflement. Her response to the most obvious question—"What's a holiday?"—was to inform us that we would be spending a week at the beach. But all that I knew of the ribbon of sand surrounding the country I lived in had been gleaned from *The Ladybird Book of the Seashore* and books about a bear named Rupert who wore tartan trousers and, when near the water's edge, came face-to-face with mermaids, discovered lost treasure in smugglers' caves, and snacked on taffy and tea cakes in picture-postcard coves and weed-wreathed grottoes.

On the morning of our departure, I was fascinated to see almost every item of clothing I owned—including some slightly effeminate ruched red swimming trunks previously donned for partial submersion in a string of inflatable paddling pools—being bundled into suitcases by Mum, who had to sit on them before they would close. A similar fate befell nearly every garment belonging to Joy, whose reaction to the news that none of her toys would be coming along for the ride had been less than favorable.

"You don't need toys at the seaside," said Mum. "Me and Dad'll buy you a bucket and spade. You'll like that."

Peevishly inferring from this revelation that Joy would be the solitary recipient of all beach-related instances of parental generosity, I immediately brought the eleven-inch guns of selfishness to maximum elevation.

"What about me?" I whined. "Don't I get a bucket and spade?"

"Of course you do, you twit. You get a bucket and spade. Joy gets a bucket and spade. You'll both have a lovely time. We'll all have a lovely time. And Auntie Jackie and Grandpa are coming with us."

Two hours later, we stepped outside into sunshine and birdsong and quietly made for the station. And, as we did so, I silently prayed that at no point in the expedition would my parents have yet another argument like the one whose words, muffled by my bedroom wall, had rendered me sleepless for most of the previous night. Yet another argument among many, many more than I could bear, yet another of the quarrels that, in time, would always remind me, even when they were relatively innocuous, of the two worst disputations, both of which left my sister and me subliminally bewildered and subconsciously shaken for decades thereafter and, I have no doubt—neither does Joy—for decades to come.

At the core of what remains of my remembrance of the first is a glimpse of a bowed and, we feared, broken Dad, inching and flinching his V-necked way toward us (Mum, at the top of the stairs, is beet-red and wielding a knife) and, through his tears, informing his petrified children that his assailant has asked him to leave. The second stands reduced to the miserable sight of my sister and me (armed, at Joy's suggestion, with plastic bows and arrows and wearing cowboy hats) desperately attempting to persuade an enraged, hysterical Mum to stop hurling plates, cups, and saucers at Dad, who had taken silent and, it turned out, inadequate refuge in the shadow of the dining room table.

VISIONS OF CATACLYSM began to recede once we arrived at Paddington, where we caught the train to Bournemouth. Striding through clouds of steam to the shrilling of whistles and the shouting of porters and guards came Grandpa. A suitcase in one hand, a nine-inch Montecristo in the other, and an antique panama on his castellated head, he was looking surreally dapper in a brand-new British Home Stores sports jacket and fiercely pressed baggy trousers, neither of which sat well with his curb-cleaving hobnails.

Tripping along behind him with what turned out to be a sizable bag of candy came Jackie, who, even on weekends, dressed for the office or a solitary night at the opera and was looking very chic that day in a cream-colored suit poised somewhere between a perfunctory glance at the New Look and a nod and a wink to Chanel. The way they were dressed on that midsummer morning, however, is something I remember with clarity only now. At the time, I'm informed, and in concert with Joy, I was thoroughly transfixed by the sight of a leviathan with six-foot wheels, three huge humps, and a tender the length of a football field.

"Is it the *Flying Scotsman*, Dad?" I yapped. "Is it? Is it? Please say yes."

"I hope not," he replied. "Because, if it is, we're stuck at the wrong flaming station."

The senescent hussar handed me a packet of Trebor Mints, lit the Montecristo, and picked up his and Jackie's cases. Dad followed suit with ours, and we walked to a carriage at what Grandpa called the "arse end" of the train.

ONCE IMPRESSED on a seat so stubbly it reminded me of my dressing gown, I greedily riffled through two comics provided by Jackie: *The Beano* (stamping ground of the Bash Street Kids, an indivisible clutch of inkpot-flinging, catapult-wielding third-graders for whom the Education Act of 1944 appeared to have done next to nothing, and Jonah, a sailor so ugly that every ship he stepped aboard sank without further ado) and *Eagle*, the paper that launched the illustrious career of an interstellar hero named Dan Dare, Pilot of the (impossibly distant) Future, whose attire, with the exception of the goldfish bowl pinned to his shoulders, bore a surprising resemblance to the dress uniform sported by RAF officers of the decidedly recent past.

SHORTLY THEREAFTER, by which time the Bash Street Kids had volunteered en masse for the roles of Brutus and Cassius in an amateur production of *Julius Caesar*, a burly man in what I now knew to be the official garb of British Rail parked an assemblage on bungled wheels next to Grandpa's metalliferous ulna and grumbled: "Tea, coffee, cake, sandwiches, biscuits."

Dad handed the sad man what looked like five bob and in return received six cups of placid tea, plus a Wagon Wheel biscuit each for Joy and me. I gobbled the biscuit with all the élan of a seasoned traveler profoundly acquainted with dining cars, swigged my tea with all the assurance of an elderly habitué of Claridge's—and thereafter dozed off, feeling a little superior for a change, with my short-back-and-sides in Jackie's lap, shielded from the sun by a wide-open copy of *Redbook*.

WHEN I WOKE UP, the train had stopped, the windows were open, and Dad and Grandpa were already outside with the cases. Mum was squirreling comics and fashion magazines into a shopping bag and scraping flattened Jelly Babies and raisins off the seats with a heavily spat-upon hankie.

Hunger pangs struck on several occasions throughout the afternoon that followed as we strolled in the hotel garden, which was bordered by drifts of flowers and ferns awash with butterflies much more kaleidoscopic than the humdrum cabbage whites in Grandpa's garden. I greeted the news, announced by Dad, that my discomfort was not to be relieved until teatime—which, he reminded me, was known as dinnertime in the part of the world we had come to—with a shrug of exasperation. A repeat performance followed five minutes later, when it emerged that a pallid Grandpa, who was smoking in a gazebo, had run out of Spangles, my favorite hard candy.

Thus deprived of gingerbread and peanut butter on toast and cold fried potatoes, to name but a few of the many interstitial treats that made my afternoons at home a paradigm of piggishness, I soon grew dissatisfied. The rot of self-pity was briefly arrested by Mum, who ran indoors, came back out brandishing *The Ladybird Book of Garden Flowers*, and proceeded to give me an unwanted snippet of quasi home-schooling in horticulture, a subject in which I have always had no interest at all. Neither the nose of the hybrid tea rose nor the bouquet of the pansy served to detach me for more than a second from the contemplation of matters of greater import, which eventually included the poached salmon that Jackie (whose peckishness I self-centeredly viewed as a welcome vindication of my own) had discovered we'd be eating at half past six. It was now half past four.

MUM NEXT SUGGESTED that we take a quick trot to the seafront, so we all trooped onto the orderly street and walked toward the line dividing Dorset from the heavens. And as we drew close to the point where the road petered out and the hairpin descent by a roundabout path to a wealth of sea levels began, the breeze picked up, and I grew aware of an ill-sated sigh twinned with a ravenous moan.

Grandpa, who was wearing binoculars snatched (as I only learned later) from the one-armed carcass of a German in

1916, picked me up and stood me on a wall covered in a carpet of lavender.

"There it is, John," billowed Mum from beneath her lime-green headscarf. "There's the sea."

The ground fell away from my feet as I gawked at the immensity, a shade of blue that seemed to have neither beginning nor end. Several seconds later, but not before Grandpa had spotted a ship as big as the *Georgic* in the distance, I fainted. (More than a decade later, Mum, having read a book on Buddhism, conjectured—laughingly at first, and then less so—that my undeniably dramatic response to this first glimpse of the sea might perhaps have had something to do with my having suffered a fatal misadventure of the maritime kind in a prior existence. This was a notion I quickly dismissed with some High Church pooh-poohing.)

FOR REASONS UNFATHOMED, my progress from Ongar to a clifftop in Dorset is all I recall of my very first outing to Bournemouth. What else I know of the sojourn is afforded by a few tableaux filmed by Dad with a secondhand cine-camera.

Attired for some reason as Little Boy Blue in matching aquamarine shorts and shirt, I am running toward the sea, sticking my big toe into what passes for surf on Albion's south coast, and then scampering back to our encampment, which consists of half a dozen deck chairs and an astonishing number of shopping bags swollen with sweaters that nobody needs because it is obviously, if only by English standards, extremely hot.

Joy, sweating in a skinny green cardigan (with daisy-shaped buttons) and marigold-yellow plastic pants, is wandering back and forth with what looks like a chocolate-flavored ice lolly.

Fast asleep with a half-smoked cigar in his mouth in the deck chair at far left is Grandpa, who, except for the fact that he has removed his shoes and socks and rolled up his trousers to midcalf, is dressed for a job interview—tie tightly knotted, white shirt starched, jacket recently dry-cleaned.

Sitting in the deck chair next to him and engrossed in a copy of *Vogue* is Jackie, decked out in what I now think of as West End come-hither reconditioned by Fellini: ivory sling-backs, Gina Lollobrigida sunglasses, and a hot-pink frock with skirts so flounced they make her look like an overblown chrysanthemum. (This was the kind of froufrou attire to which Mum took silent exception, particularly when it was being worn by my aunt, on whom Grandma and Grandpa had, relatively speaking, lavished more affection than they ever had on Mum or departed Aunt Betty.)

Next in line is the deck chair vacated by the auteur of the piece.

Then comes the deck chair snaring Mum. She is furiously brushing sand out of my hair while keeping an eye on Joy, who has tottered back into shot with her pants around her ankles.

The scene now shifts to a day so bright that Grandpa has loosened his tie, Jackie has donned a bikini, and Dad—sporting baggy swimming trunks, a singlet with several holes in it, and a gray cloth cap—is applying calamine lotion to his squinting children, who are up to their waists in a trench in the sand and wearing conical hats.

Next, Grandpa is sitting on a bench with Joy (who is eating cotton candy) beside an Olympic-size paddling pool dotted with hundreds of toddlers brandishing pinwheels and fishing nets. Both Grandpa and Joy look radiant.

In the final scene, Grandpa is sitting on the same bench with me on his lap. We are both looking straight at the camera. I am smiling—a little uncertainly—and wielding an ice cream. Grandpa, his face as expressionless as it later stayed throughout a BBC broadcast of *Paths of Glory,* is holding a half-eaten sandwich.

PART TWO

....

a nice cup of tea and a biscuit

Watching a Punch and Judy
show in Ongar, 1959

CHAPTER 4

A Pipsqueak of Marmalade

. . . .

BY THE MIDDLE OF 1959, WHEN I WAS FIVE, THE HOUSING ES-
tate on which we lived, like all the others in Ongar, was filling
up fast, and I had begun to notice not only that none of our
neighbors had a car as senile as the Austin but also that my
brand-new Hornby train set—a single locomotive, a single
carriage, a circle of track less than four feet in diameter, and a
middle-of-nowhere platform that I had chosen to populate
with a plastic lion, a tin grizzly bear, and a twig standing in
for a tree—was simply no match for the considerably more
expensive (and near-transcontinental) Tri-ang assemblages
owned by quite a number of my neighborhood friends.

These disparities were, however, of a merely material nature, and not quite sufficient, just yet, to allow the word
"class"—which I'd originally heard used when Dad first tried
to tell me what it was that most distinguished the Isle of Dogs
from other parts of London and the world—to reverberate
within my little brain with anything like authority. They were

also largely, but not completely, compensated for, as far as I was concerned, by the uniform nature of our play, which mostly consisted of stirring reenactments (with toy guns, tanks, airplanes, and battleships) of half-digested stories of battles fought by brothers and uncles who never returned, by Desert Rats, the RAF, the Royal Marines, and the Navy, who always won in a foursquare fight against those sausage-eating gits we all knew as Squareheads, Krauts, Huns, Blond Bastards, Jerry, and, if we were feeling less inflamed, the Germans.

The joys (such as they were) of these activities did nothing, however, to alleviate the anguish that attended our awareness of the fact that we would soon be starting school. As summer sullenly dwindled into downpours, the disappearance of raspberry-ripple ice cream, and the advent of sway-backed coal trucks manned by sooty misanthropes, we talked less of war and more about the contradictory intelligence we had received at irregular intervals throughout the previous year from a six-year-old thug named Nigel.

Had we realized then that Nigel's critiques of Ongar Primary School had more to do with his own deficiencies than they did with those of the teachers, we would have viewed the more palpable dangers of compulsory education—which, according to Nigel, required a certain willingness on the part of its recipients to play dead when denounced as "dimwit," "dunce," and "slowcoach"—with more equanimity.

DURING THIS SAME PERIOD, Mum, who wasn't entirely convinced that my formal education would necessarily give me the appreciable and all-important advantage over my peers that she so badly wanted me to have, had begun to encourage me to spend as much time as I could at the houses of certain neighbors who were what would then have been called "a cut above us" not only economically but—which was always quite a bit more to the point, in Mum's eyes—also intellectually. Even though I was only now beginning to read, Mum, desperately focused on what I think she hoped would be an erudite and eminent future, aimed me unerringly at the local intelligentsia.

The first of the targeted houses concerned was the right-hand half, when you faced it, of the semidetached that stood to the left of ours. It was always thoughtfully occupied by the Burgess family—Matthew (my primary playmate), Jane (his mum), and Julian ("Mr. Burgess" to me), his Guinness-swilling dad. Mr. Burgess's career and extracurricular interests read like a character outline Simon Raven might have sketched while working on *Alms for Oblivion*—scion of a seafaring family, product of the Royal Naval College (in Dartmouth), prewar Fleet Air Arm torpedo specialist, diving instructor during World War II, author of several reasonably well-reviewed detective novels, and, since 1946, account executive at an advertising agency. Jane had worked in New York for the British Ministry of Information during the war, subscribed to *The New Yorker*, and would later lend Mum novels by Mary McCarthy and poetry by Marianne Moore and William Carlos Williams. Matthew, who was my age and a prodigy of sorts, never dropped his aitches, in winter wore a duffle coat (never gabardine), already understood the rules of chess, and was thinking of taking up the trumpet. The Burgesses' entire living room was walled with books.

Jane Burgess's parents, Philip and Cecily Skipton, lived in

the second house on Mum's hit list. They had recently retired from a combined total of eighty years of teaching in East End elementary schools, owned rental properties in a part of the East End called Poplar, made a mean gin and vermouth (a drink Mum thought a bit out of her league but never said no to at Christmas), and spent the hours that circled their sundial in daylight reciting Kipling and Shakespeare from memory in a sitting room dominated by a bust of Beethoven, a statuette of Socrates, a picture of Edith Sitwell, and a photograph of William Walton snapped backstage, they said, at an amateur production of *Belshazzar's Feast*. The Skiptons' living room was also lined with bookshelves, as was one wall of their bedroom.

Location number three in Mum's plan of attack, a fully detached Bauhausian manse set back from the High Street, was peopled by the Ramsays and completely cluttered—hallway, stairway, landing, lavatories, living room, dining room, cavernous bathroom, and each and every windowsill—with books. The head of the household, Edward Ramsay, the son of a Lancashire miner, had a master's degree in English from the University of London, taught at a Catholic high school in nearby Chelmsford, and had recently signed a contract with Oxford University Press for what turned out to be a well-regarded monograph on the poems of Thomas Hardy. His wife, Eleanor, the money behind the mayhem, came from a long line of doctors and financiers and had received her secondary education at one of the most unconventional fee-paying schools in the country, a highly progressive establishment that barely had a curriculum and, as Mum once said very wistfully many years later while smoking a Gitane filched from Joy, "encouraged self-expression." (Eleanor Ramsay was also a Cordon Bleu–trained cook but preferred to fatten her tribe on nothing more exotic than perfunctory fry-ups.) Her perpetually disheveled and runny-nosed progeny—Timothy, Peter, and Ann, all of whom would also attend unusual and not inexpensive schools—were expert tobogganists and fiendishly fond of fresh air.

Domicile number four, which, by the skin of its bricks, was connected to ours, wore its learning and flourishes more lightly. The book selection was largely confined to Thackeray, Fielding, Wilkie Collins, Trollope, and the Brontës; the record collection to Chopin and Schubert; the heirloom glass to Rosenthal; the china to Meissen; the clocks to ormolu. Amid these examples of tightly focused taste sat Jennifer Walsh, whose husband, a lieutenant commander in the Navy, had recently been felled by a heart attack at the age of fifty-two.

Jennifer, whose concept of cuisine was nowhere near as elegant as her taste in literature, lived largely on cookies and uninspired salads, played the piano every afternoon, and nursed any birds that Twinkle, our third ill-fated feline (two had died young in the space of a year), had caught but failed to puncture to the point of no return. She was infinitely kind to the youngest Haneys and so gracious and polite to their parents that Dad could never stand easy in her presence but came to attention with parade-ground alacrity whenever she tapped at our back-door window to ask if she might borrow a spoonful of sugar or a couple of slices of bread until tomorrow. And the most memorable hours, perhaps, of those sweetened and starched thereafters—at least to my way of thinking then and, surprisingly often, now—followed an anthracite-

With Joy in Ongar, 1960

heated evening in September 1959, on the day before I started school.

ENGLAND'S RIGHTS and Germany's wrongs faded from view as Mum, who was angry with Dad about something, allowed me to overload on white toast and jam while she read to me, from a book I could barely begin to manage, about the childhood of Elizabeth I. Twinkle was peaceably sharing a wing chair with a wide-eyed but uninvolved Joy. Dad, who was keeping out of the way, had retreated to the dining room and, having recorded our income and outgo for the previous week in a notebook he'd nicked from the office, was now playing "Jesu, Joy of Man's Desiring" over and over again very slowly on our chronically untuned piano.

At nine o'clock, I went up to bed. Eleven hours later, I fumbled awake, got dressed in seconds, and ran at a *William Tell Overture* clip all the way down the uncarpeted (another of Mum's many bones of contention) stairs. Upon my arrival in the kitchen, Mum gave me two slices of bread and butter and a tub of Canadian honey. Half an hour later, the ringing of the doorbell announced the arrival of my friend David Allport and his mum, Auntie Julia, whose brother (and the Hurricane he was flying at the time) had been battered to bits—said David's dad, Mike, who was something quite senior in banking and drove a Jag—a few thousand feet above Folkestone in 1940.

DAVID AND I EVENTUALLY became Ongar Primary School's least corrigible chatterboxes, but in our demeanor en route to our first day there, we matched the average Trappist. When we got to school, David's mum gave him a hug. Mum, who had Joy in her arms, gave me a lipsticky kiss. David and I were then gently but firmly herded, along with forty other children, into the school's assembly hall. On a platform at one end stood the headmaster, Mr. Harker, whose sobering suit stood in some contra-rotation to the regimental splendor of his tie.

Outflanking him were half a dozen females and a bullish-looking male with a Pleistocene stare and the build of a sack of cement. Two of the women, smiling too sweetly in solid-colored dresses (washed out bottle-green in one case, marigold in the other), were young and fairly attractive. Three of them, cut from less cordial cloth, were florally overthrown frumps.

The sixth of the females frightened me the second I saw her: she looked like a drainpipe decked out in field gray. Her nose could have passed for a stonemason's chisel and her eyes in their cavities glimmered like guttering candles. Her name was Eileen O'Rourke, and I eventually learned that she was a remarkable teacher who treated children as equals and loved to make them laugh.

The sack of cement stood out from the crowd by virtue of the madness of his wardrobe: forest-green jacket, light blue trousers, orange-and-turquoise diamond-patterned V-neck, canary-yellow shirt, and chocolate tie. (This was Mr. Underwood, a "bit of a brute," according to Mum; he taught the remedial class.)

We were then led away to a classroom.

AT ELEVEN O'CLOCK, we broke for "lunch": a little milk donated by the government, plus snacks we'd brought from home. I dutifully guzzled my unlovely biscuits—a flavorless brand called Nice that I loathed—and swallowed my milk in a single glug. Next, we mixed up powder paints and I composed a poorly proportioned full-length portrait of Mum that made her look less like a slender brunette in a white summer dress with a motif of tiny roses and more like a bloodspattered Moomintroll with a runaway case of the mumps.

By twelve o'clock my ability to pay attention had been undone by hunger, and the declaration of dinnertime came as an appreciable relief. We filed across the playground to a monumental biscuit tin, an edifice—painted a black-hearted hue of dark green—that I now remember, still fondly, as a paramount shrine to amoebic meat and limitless processed (also called "cannonball") peas. The moment the midday bell resounded, my heart would leap at the thought of skipping across the potholed tarmac to the land of beef and treacle, the hallowed spot where half a dozen of the muscular wives and lumpy mothers of Ongar's least well paid inhabitants (road menders, street sweepers, dustmen, and farmhands) struggled in limited space to produce, with the aid of equipment that had probably been installed in the 1930s, something resembling dinner for nearly three hundred infants.

The meal to which I most looked forward was a version of Lancashire hotpot that looked and tasted nothing like the dish of the same name described by the editor of *McCall's Introduction to British Cooking,* published that same year on the other side of the Atlantic. Hotpot's incarnation at Ongar Primary substituted neck of grizzled sheep for nicely trimmed chops of hitherto gamboling lamb, sent the cream to Coventry, replaced the bovine consommé with Bovril-tainted tap water, left as many black spots as possible in the spuds, ignored the onions, and gave the parsley sprigs the heave-ho. The result was a crock of aged ruminant—even now I remember its taste with relish—queasily suspended in blobs of grease beneath an uneven mosaic of blistered potato.

And what of the sweet tooth, the sad predilection for sugar that has busied generations of British dentists? Beneath the lid of the biscuit tin, its first satisfaction was primarily ensured by rivers of packet-mix yellow custard. Yellow custard's gooey doppelgänger, pink custard, was usually served with a square of granite shortbread whose reduction to manageable pieces frequently required the tiny diner to stand semierect, take hold of a fork or a spoon with both claws, apply the implement to the center of the biscuit, and then, keeping his or her arms straight, lean forward. On a good day, the shortbread crumbled with a minimum of protest. On a bad one, it streaked across the room in a thousand pieces to a chorus of impish caterwauls and other typically British expressions of schadenfreude.

WHEN LOOKING BACK on my first three years at school, I'm struck by how very well Ongar Primary's pupils "mucked in together," as Dad would have put it, despite their economic differences. (He always thought of "mucking in" as the flagship reverse of his greatest dislikes: one-upmanship, elitism, and snobbery.)

Some of us wore clothes so heavily darned that an astonishing fraction of the original fabric had been obscured by snaky traces of cotton thread that resembled the imprint of stitches. Others wore garments emblematic of the hours their mothers had spent dragging their offspring through the clothing sections of midprice department stores in the capital's northeastern suburbs. But we were all friends by and large, and if the lives we led in that land of relative contentment had been the subject of a documentary, the opening movement of Beethoven's Sixth would have been a reasonably cerebral choice of sound track.

Something less uplifting, however—Schoenberg springs to mind—would have been required to convey the tenor of life at No. 13 Mayflower Way, where Dad, to Mum's continuing annoyance, remained set in his steady-job ways. Which

At Ongar Primary, 1963

was one reason why she now redoubled her efforts to subject Joy and me to the (at-home) intellectual force-feeding she assumed (not entirely incorrectly) to have been inflicted on the Ramsay children and Matthew because their parents were university educated. The genteel wreckage of landed Scotland was still at war with the modest expectations of London's East End.

THE COST OF READING ROCKETED—to Dad's mild and impotent dismay—as hardback editions of quality books like *The*

Ship That Flew, Charlotte's Web, and *The Witch of Blackbird Pond* obliterated every trace of Enid Blyton, at that time England's preeminent author of boilerplate fictions for under-thirteens. The additional expenditure (further exacerbated by increased outlays on clothes and cultural excursions) caused further arguments. To make things even worse from my point of view, we now saw almost nothing of the Romford and Rayleigh East Enders (perhaps because Dick, Dad, and Dave saw enough of each other at work) and even less of Ray and Eileen, or of Rose (who had now given birth to two girls) and Uncle Don.

Shrinking from the shadows cast by dissonance at home and by the loss of the genuine laughter I had grown to associate solely with the unassuming, unpretentious Cockneys, I fled to my Puffins and quickly emerged as a shortsighted reader of tales of Trojans, of Dido's passion for fickle Aeneas, of Lancelot's laying of perilous siege to the fluttering heart of a sad queen called Guinevere, and of daring escapes from Colditz. Joy began school and did drawings that her teachers took quite seriously at first. And Mum got a job at an estate agent's office in the wake of our second (and last) expedition to Bournemouth, a seven-day sojourn that cost Dad, otherwise the safely grounded genius of frugality, the equivalent of an entire month's salary plus overtime, most of it—this did not surprise me when I found out, many years later—simply borrowed.

The recently expired Austin Seven had been replaced by an equally sickly Austin Eight, and in it we drove, in August 1962—I was now eight; Joy was six—at low speed through London and not a lot faster on highways and byways that led ever farther southwest. Joy and I sat between waking and sleeping as the miles disappeared and Mum and Dad said less and less—which made me increasingly listless—until late afternoon turned to early evening and journey's end in the gravel driveway of Cliffside, a superior guesthouse owned by a man named Mr. Pitt, previously a partner (and, Mum noted, head chef) at the partly remembered hotel with gazebo where Grandpa, all behemoth boots and duckboard jacket, ran out of Spangles but never cigars.

We entered a world—or so it seemed to eyes as untrained as those of small people from Essex—of immaculate décor, of white linen tablecloths and certified silverware. We were now above stairs, in a manner of speaking, in a manicured mini-mansion where children were supposed never to speak unless spoken to first and the adults conversed in the kind of hushed tones usually reserved for a missile crisis. (Years were to pass before I realized that Cliffside hadn't been particularly grand.) And even though the weather was warm and the sun had been shining all day and I—for some undoubtedly not quite rational, Mum-rooted reason that escapes me and, unlike Joy, who was wearing a sundress—was oddly over-clothed in long socks, vest, flannel shirt, and V-neck sweater, I found myself, within minutes of our arrival, feeling detectably chilled.

"This is a bit smart, isn't it, Mum?" I asked as she unpacked. (Dad, who was in Mum's bad books yet again, had sloped off for a smoke outside, taking Joy with him.)

"Not really, dear. It's a little bit nicer than the Hillcrest Dene. But I think we deserve it."

"Deserve it? What for?" (In her worst moods, Mum had a habit of telling my sister and me that we were thoroughly ungrateful and deserved absolutely nothing. Dad, I knew, disagreed, but did "fuck-all," which he never said in front of Joy, to stop her.)

"Well, me and your dad have been working. Working very hard. As I very much hope you've noticed."

"I have," I said, suddenly feeling extremely dejected and not un-inclined to show it.

"Please don't start moping, John."

"I'm sorry."

"We've come here to have a nice time."

"I know."

BREAKFAST ON OUR FIRST DAY there was a minor's revelation, my earliest exposure to a mode of eating preferred by gentle-folk. Sitting up desperately straight in stiff chairs, Joy and I stared in some confusion (and with just a little anxiety) at the elaborately folded napkins and watched with suspicion as a waitress dictated a couplet that sounded like "fruit juice." A few minutes later, four supremely un-smudged glasses of yellow stuff arrived.

The sip I took, and the face I pulled, precipitated a talking-to in whispers. Grapefruit juice—this was the unsweetened kind—I learned from Mum, came from grapefruit (which I'd never had) in much the same way that orange squash, which we bought from a milkman who also sold eggs and whose destroyer had been hit by ("of all things," he chirruped despite his Falstaffian girth) a tank shell on D-Day, came from oranges. The juice also had to be consumed before one ate one's Krispies, which came without milk (or so it appeared to me, until I learned the meaning of "milk jug") in a low bowl with something Mum called a hallmark on its apparently quite refined bottom. A cup of tea and a slice of toast, the two-pronged *amuse-gueule* of breakfast in Ongar, were out of the question until every jot of juice and tittle of Krispies were well on their way to one's stomach. And jam was to be spooned onto bread, rather than scraped from the jar with a buttery knife.

Once the tea and toast turned up, I swigged and bit to my heart's content and thought about Florence Nightingale, bikinis, and astronomy. Then, just as I was about to ask whether I might be allowed to get down, Mr. Pitt's daughter, Nicola, who wore very short shorts and was taller than Dad, presented me with a heart-stopping glimpse of her velvety suntanned thighs and two more slices of toast, this time studded with things that reminded me of very large rabbit scat and also of the spicy lumps of a sausage called chorizo that Grandpa had once been given by his Spanish neighbors, Luís and Pilar Alvarez.

I looked up at Dad, who was leafing through yesterday's *Guardian*, and then at Mum, who said: "Kidneys. From a cow, dear. You've had them in steak and kidney pie. It's just that. Well. On toast. They're not chopped up. I think you'll like them."

The day of discovery continued, the strangeness of breakfast (and lunch, as it turned out) somehow overshadowing the hours we spent at the beach, where Joy and I made sand castles with help from Dad while Mum, fortified by choc ices, plodded through one of three thin Penguins—"Puffins for grown-ups," Phil Skipton had quipped—by Henry James.

At noon, we trickled back to our rooms, where Joy and I traded in our bathing suits for crisply pressed shorts and shirts. Mum put on one of her least frumpy frocks, and Dad

With Mum, Dad, and Joy, 1967

wore a jacket and tie. Then we filed into the dining room, where things got off to an inauspicious start courtesy of my introduction to a substance called tomato juice, which made me gag first, then sneeze, and finally drop my glass into my lap. In the absence of a napkin, the juice took the path of least resistance, squishing between my legs and fanning out left, right, and center beneath me and onto the carpet.

This event caused a tremendous stir among the salon's other occupants. I was stared at—which made me shrivel—by four fat old men with lollipop faces and floss of white hair, a plague of archaic ladies whose cumbersome feet and waspish torsos made them look like triffids, the (very) few (and undoubtedly overextended) people who looked like us, two young men with polio, and a spastic in her teens with a lopsided smile that I thought profoundly appealing.

Dad pretended not to notice. Joy, who also had her doubts about the juice, discreetly spat hers back into the glass. The retired Indian Army officers (as Mum found out later they were) tucked back into their curry, the triffids synchronized watches, the men with matchstick lower limbs returned to their mountainous salads, the uneven smile grew wider. Mum, for her part, having had considerable experience of similar mishaps, got me upstairs, undressed, softly soaped, and newly presentable in minutes.

"I'm sorry, Mum," I sniveled.

"It's all right, dear. It's not your fault. Really."

"I don't think I like tomato juice."

"I can see that," she said, with her least anxious laugh of the day.

"I won't have to have it again, will I?"

"Not if you don't like it. No. Of course not."

"Are we going back downstairs now? Or do we have to stay here?"

"What on earth do you mean, dear? Of course we're going back down."

"But those other people were giving us funny looks, Mum."

"Don't be silly."

"They were."

"No, they weren't."

"Yes, they were," I almost shouted, sensing a first sting of tears. "Everyone's so posh here. Hardly anybody talks to us, Mum."

"Stop it, John. They were *not* giving us funny looks. And it's not *that* posh. And if people want to keep themselves to themselves—well, they can. So you can stop all this nonsense, hear me? We'll finish our lunch. And then we'll go back to the beach."

"It *is* posh," I protested, reeling from a speedily evolving conviction that there were definitely two distinct species of posh: one that came with kindness and civility (Eleanor Ramsay, Jennifer Walsh, the Burgesses, the Skiptons) and another that came without (far too many people at the place where we were staying). "I saw two blokes laughing at our car."

Mum's face fell.

"Your father worked hard for that car, John. It may not be much, but it gets us around."

"I know."

I was now feeling tired and depressed.

"Come on, then. Dinner's getting cold. Dad and Joy'll be wondering what's wrong."

"What's *Washington Square* about, Mum?"

"Oh. I don't know. Some of it's about love. And people being—well—a bit disappointed."

AFTER I'D BEEN repositioned at the table, Nicola Pitt, whose immortal thighs had now decamped to a dark skirt at odds with the antics of morning, brought me a helping of something I enjoyed enormously—chicken pie, which kept me quiet for nearly fifteen minutes once I had managed to tear myself away from the sight of her sublimely symmetrical backside as it sailed toward the kitchen's swing doors. Then dessert arrived, in the form of ice cream and a peach, which—as Mum informed me with a look of approval that might have

been scripted by Elizabeth David—was apparently "fresh."
Inwardly bemoaning the absence of syrup, I speared a morsel,
chewed it once, winced twice, and, as quietly as I could, expelled it.

Several mouthfuls of seawater and far too much cotton
candy later, Joy and I were given a good cleaning (Joy's third
and my fourth of the day) by Mum and taken for a pre-dinner
ramble the length and breadth of the gardens, the croquet
lawn, and the putting green. To my relief, we did not bring
the Ladybird book about flowers. Dad quietly absconded to a
deck chair on the porch with a packet of Woodbines and the
last few pages of a cinder block entitled *Hawaii*, which Mum
had excoriated earlier in the afternoon while taking a breather
from, as Auntie Jane later described it to me, the analysis of
deceit that makes *The Aspern Papers* so much more disturbing
than any of the vileness in *The Turn of the Screw*. Among the
sights we saw in a quick succession of zigzags were a waiter
kissing a waitress, a rodent rotting greenly in a cistern, and a
bony dog in hot pursuit of a honey-colored butterfly.

When we returned to the patio, Dad had finished *Hawaii*,
exchanged it for a discarded copy of the *Daily Express*, and
persuaded a wandering waitress (who seemed, he told Mum,
to be walking on air) to bring him a cup of tea. At which
point, I rudely interrupted and begged—as I had five times a
week, he often said—to be regaled with orphanage stories
and maybe some tales told much more than twice about life in
the Blitz and the Army. Mum walked off to talk to the Burtons, a couple from Yorkshire we'd met at lunch: Mrs. Bur-
ton, who worked as a nurse at a home for retarded children
and was married to a Low Church Anglican vicar (and war-

time chaplain) who had lost half an arm at Dunkirk, had assisted in my rescue from the tempest of juice.

DAD OFTEN PREFACED his less than methodical discourses on
his years at the Alexandra Orphanage with a distant memory
of sitting with several other tots in a pram the size of a row-
boat and being wheeled around places he later knew as
Haverstock Hill and portions of Hampstead Heath. The food,
he said, was uniformly awful from 1926, when Nana Haney
carried him there, until 1935, when, in one and the same week,
the matron suffered a heart attack and the headmistress was
run over by a tram. This coincidence ushered in a new and
more enlightened administration, which sacked the head cook
and complained to the treasurer, who pumped a few more
pennies into the system whose finance he managed when he
wasn't making millions in the flour business.

The early days, when Dad was still learning to walk,
were marred by breakfasts consisting of nothing but aerated
bread and a pipsqueak of marmalade or maybe a basin of watery cocoa. Marmite put in an appearance at irregular intervals; tea was not forthcoming until the tram had done its
worst. At about the age of four, Dad was put on the "porridge list," as were all the spindly infants, and was also given
a daily dose of cod liver oil, prescribed by the long-faced
Harley Street doctor who visited once a month. This substance was almost as revolting as its semilethal relative, cas-
tor oil, which was supposedly a remedy for everything from
whooping cough to colic and sometimes had the dire effect,
as Dad described it to my excremental glee, of opening up
the sluices at both ends. ("You didn't stick your hand up

when that stuff went through you," he said. "You ran like the clappers.")

Sabbaths were especially unpleasant under the old regime, since the kitchen staff had the day off. With luck, one saw a slice of corned beef, a hot potato sullenly cooked by the janitor, and a very thin slice of tinned beet. The Lord's Day was also a big disappointment in the department that covered such favorite things as "pudding," "sweet," "afters," and "duff." (Dad never called it dessert.) Mondays, at least, brought enough boiled beef (but no carrots) to make everyone belch. Tuesday saw an improvement on Sunday's starvation, too: to Argentine ox parts and purplish root (but not to the plate they were served on) was added a measly slice of spotted dick (a pudding cudgeled from currants and suet and now and then garnished with custard). Thus also went Wednesdays and Thursdays and Saturdays, with Fridays reserved for fish.

The only Sundays the orphans enjoyed from 1935 onward were the ones that entailed an annual pilgrimage, aboard a fleet of charabancs, to an estate on the Thames owned by a charitable aristocrat. The children got to play in the grounds and gorge themselves on as many bowls of strawberries and cream as they wanted. But the sting in the tail of all this ducal munificence was as ghastly as a hornet's. Unaccustomed to food so rich, almost every child and the occasional teacher were horribly sick "all over the bloody place" while journeying home. Dad always said this with a cough that now makes me wonder whether reportage had reeled him in uncomfortably close to reliving.

Here the story ended, three hours before sunset, in Bournemouth, on the day that included my first exposure to untrammeled vitamin C. The dinner gong sounded. Mum returned from her chat with the Burtons. Dad collected his thoughts, his book, and his teacup.

"Orphanage stories?" said Mum.

"Yes," I replied rather dully, not knowing, once again, whether to giggle or weep at the Janus-faced thought of the hardier kids, with fruit-flavored breath, scenting a swamp, on chartered wheels, of inescapable vomit.

"War stories, too?" she continued.

"No, Mum—not today."

NOW HANDY WITH A napkin and slightly buoyed by the knowledge that my very first sips of tomato juice had also been my last, I managed the preliminaries (a small tin of Cydrax) with immodest aplomb. The next course turned out to be an unfamiliar fish.

"What is it, Mum?"

"Dover sole."

"Is it from Dover?"

"Not always."

"What's this?"

"It's a fish knife."

"What? Just for fish?"

"Yes," said Dad, a little, I later thought, bitterly. "Just for fish. They do things properly here."

I harpooned a portion, dipped it in the sauce, and thrust it into my mouth. It was better—so much better—than anything Birdseye, better than Mum's disquieted fish sticks, better than the sardines I could barely remember having had (along with a packet of chocolate biscuits) at Nana Haney's, better than Grandma's prickly cod, better than Grandpa's kip-

With Nana Haney and Joy in Plaistow, 1957

pers, haddock, and whitebait. Better than any of the flatulent
fish that came with wet chips in Ongar, better than rock eel
and plaice. Or maybe not better. Just different.

I was still pursuing this tormented line of thought when,
having ransacked an apple galette, we adjourned to the
lounge, where the officers sat at one end of the room and
played cards and the alien plant life huddled at the other and
flicked through *Town and Country* and the *Tatler*. Mum and
Dad and Joy and I sat somewhere in the middle, on a sofa. Silence blossomed. Dad and I looked at our shoes. Mum surveyed the contents of her handbag. Joy, stuffed with sole and

a huge second helping of Mr. Pitt's third course, dozed off and began to drool.

The fact that it was now so very quiet in the place of withdrawal that the ticking of the grandfather clock in the hallway was as audible as Mrs. O'Rourke in mid-cackle made the sudden arrival of Nicola Pitt at the overwrought helm of a coffee-cart-cum-cake-and-biscuit-stand so ear-shattering that she might just as well have been driving a half-track across the Iranian carpet. Expecting a chocolate finger and a mug of lukewarm Nescafé, I was confused in an instant when she handed me a small éclair and a piddling cup (with impractical handle) of a liquid as black as the everlasting oil slick on the floor of our garage.

"Would you like some cream in that, young man?"

"Isn't there any milk?" (Cream, as far as I knew, came from a tin and was purely for adding to apple pie, tinned pear halves, super-chilled prunes, and canned peaches.)

"It's nicer with cream."

"Thank you very much."

"Sugar?"

"Yes, please."

It was brown. I decided not to say anything and simply stirred away at the contents of the cup until the last swirl of cream had blended with the permanent stain and every last crystal of sugar had dissolved. I took a sip and, stupefied, smiled.

I ignored the microscopic éclair, settled back against the brocade, drained my coffee, and asked for more. Dad, who was biting his nails, asked for more tea. When it arrived, he drank it quickly, put down his cup, and went back to staring rather sadly at his shoes. Mum lunged at Joy, who was on the verge of falling off the couch.

THE NEXT SIX DAYS were devoid of disaster. By the time we left, I knew that among the things—the very few things— I would miss about Bournemouth, which I seemed to have liked (according to the cine-film) well enough when I was younger, were Mr. Pitt's coffee, his daughter's dimensions, and the kindness of the Burtons, who had the best manners I had yet, in my short life, encountered. They had taken Joy and me for circular strolls in the clifftop gardens and for heavenly walks on the beach—where Mr. B. sang the psalms he knew by heart to indifferent seagulls—while Mum discerned *What Maisie Knew* and said little to Dad, who, in the wake of a trip to a secondhand bookstore in Poole, smoked his way, unattended and slowly, first through *The War of the Worlds* and then *The Invisible Man*.

We never went back to Bournemouth, and most of what I sensed there still makes me want to give it a wide berth today.

CHAPTER 5

High-Speed Burnt Toast and Fake Coffee

. . . .

BY THE MIDDLE OF 1964, JOY, WHO HAD STARTED SCHOOL IN 1961 and was now in the remedial class, was in a state of continual misery that, it seemed, no amount of ballet lessons or trips to the movies could even begin to allay. Her abilities with a paintbrush and snip-snaps of charcoal had not been matched by commensurate artifice where reading, writing, and arithmetic were concerned. I, on the other hand, was moderately happy spending most of my spare time reading. My texts spanned the gamut, at No. 13, from the inevitable comics and other "junk" (to quote Mum) of what Dad liked to call the "thud and blunder" kind to a Zion (in Mum's eyes) of the pedigreed imagination, an eminence of reverie overrun by roving bands of Puffins (*Peter Pan, The Midnight Folk, Kidnapped, Five Children and It*).

At the Ramsays', I tranquilly mauled clusters of Penguins and squadrons of Pelicans. At the Burgesses', I attempted to ingest an assortment of volumes I could barely comprehend but felt obliged to rummage through as if mere exposure, mere plodding acquaintance, might ensure my arrival, in time, at the Xanadu of broad-based understanding. My struggles took in *Lord Weary's Castle* (as Jane said later, this, like most of Lowell, starts where manic depression stops), Larkin's *The North Ship*, and Auden and Isherwood's *Ascent of F6*.

I WAS, IN ESSENCE, being schooled in other people's houses, and especially chez Burgess, perhaps because, as I eventually came to suspect and did not particularly appreciate, Mum rather hoped I would one day grow up to be Matthew. And it was also at the Burgesses' house that I first came to realize—nose thinking, tongue twitching, all teeth engaged—that there was more to food than gingerbread and bangers.

The Burgesses' culinary proclivities were a mix of the pedestrian (fish fingers, tinned spaghetti), the putatively healthful (yogurt, Ryvita), and, beginning in the autumn of 1964, when Mr. Burgess began to think about visiting France, the fetid, a kind of food that Joy refused to touch until her late teens and I decided to tolerate because it was, after all, a bit posh and might therefore be approved of by Mum.

The most palpable turn of the tide in the nature of my relationship with the food on offer on what Joy called stink-bomb night at the Burgesses' came on a Sunday in the spring of '65. She made do with ham and eggs while the rest of us corroded a pistachio-stippled pork pâté and a huddle of cheeses from Harrods. As the evening wore on, and despite the fact that I genuinely liked the Burgesses' company, I found myself thinking of Dad's exhausted arrivals and drowsy departures, the barely perceptible tightening (which worried me) of his smile. I wondered how he felt when visited, as he was at random, by what I now knew was his earliest memory of the orphanage. This memory predated the perambulator on Haverstock Hill; it not only reinforced my misgivings concerning happiness but also left me with a nagging sense of exile and exclusion that was destined to persist. It was Mum who had told me about it, over weak tea and raspberry wafers on our final day in Dorset, when Dad and Joy were asleep in adjoining deck chairs: a terrified Dad, eighteen months old, is sitting in an agony of unaccustomed solitude at the foot of a vast flight of underlit stairs and screaming as Nana Haney's departing footsteps echo from stone-cold floor to invisible ceiling and fade.

The needlepoint sourness of the note thus struck returned me in an instant to the comforts of the present, to a time and a place where strawberries never spelled disaster. Finally, moments before our farewells, I swallowed (and very much enjoyed) what was left of the Roquefort, a cheese I had greatly disdained the first time I tried it.

"Well," said Mr. Burgess, looking up from *Phèdre,* "you'll be singing 'Sur le Pont' in no time."

TOWARD THE END of 1964, my thirty-nine classmates and I were reminded of the fact that in a few months' time we would be taking the examination known as the Eleven Plus. Those who passed would go on to grammar school or technical high school; those who failed would find themselves at the local secondary modern, regarded by all who avoided it as the educational equivalent of a garbage heap and known, ironi-

cally, as Top School by virtue of its location at what Ongari-
ans referred to as the top of the village. (It was also known as
the Dump.)

As the day of reckoning slithered into view, Mum repeatedly told me that my teacher, the formidably educated (including Ancient Hebrew) Mrs. Evans, thought that if I got
into grammar school I should slog with a conscience at Latin
and slave away at Greek. Soon, there came an invitation (not
to be refused) to sit an exam for a scholarship to a fee-paying
school in nearby Brentwood if I passed the Eleven Plus,
which, early in 1965, I did.

SHORTLY THEREAFTER, at eight in the morning on a Saturday
in May, my parents and I, in our Sunday best, piled into our
latest jalopy—a fourth-hand Ford Prefect with mystified
brakes, nonperforming shock absorbers, and a cracked and
easily dislodged rearview mirror—for the six-mile drive to
Brentwood. Only when we drove through the gates of the
school did I deign to pay attention to my surroundings, setting aside Alan Garner's *The Weirdstone of Brisingamen* and
affrightedly spotting the unsettled presence of astringent-
looking late-middle-aged men in an ebb and dark flow of
black gowns.

Once we were out of the car, Mum, for the fifteenth time
since breakfast—high-speed burnt toast and fake coffee—
straightened my tie, brushed imaginary lint from my jacket, and
scrubbed several microns of skin from my hands, knees, and
ears with the aid of a spat-upon hankie. Brutally clean, hopelessly whey-faced, decidedly jumpy, and wincing, I followed
Mum and Dad into a wood-paneled hall that contained still

more potential inquisitors, maybe a hundred and fifty eleven-year-olds of my own ilk, including David and five other boys from Ongar Primary, and a clutch of athletic-looking big boys who radiated boundless authority and a seemingly instinctive, completely intimidating hauteur. The capo of these janissaries began to intone the names of the candidates, who stepped forward to be marshaled into groups of thirty or so and marched off to a classroom by one of his fellow subalterns in silence.

Once we were seated, the prefect withdrew, to be replaced by a master who looked at us disapprovingly, pursed his lips, gazed at the clock on the wall for what seemed like an eternity as we fiddled with our fountain pens, and finally said: "You may begin . . . *now.*"

The Brentwood exam made the Eleven Plus look like a spelling test containing words of no more than three characters. Mired in despair from the outset, I sweated for two long hours, almost, but not quite, utterly out of my depth.

"If I fail this exam," I reasoned to myself as I sparred with sadistically difficult fractions, "I'll be going to a school that the people at this school look at the way me and my friends look at Top School. Which means, I suppose, that even though I'll be going to a 'good school,' it won't be the best school. So I'll be a success—and a failure."

"Please stop writing. . . . That means all of you. . . . Put that pen *down*, boy, are you deaf? What's your name?"

"Allport, sir," squeaked David.

TWO WEEKS LATER, I was playing in a game of football refereed by Mrs. Evans and reveling in my brand-new secondhand soccer boots, which I had bullied Mum into buying at a jumble sale. Neither side had scored a goal, and neither side much cared.

Moments before half-time, Mr. Harker, tie ablaze and trousers pressed, asked the boys who had taken the Brentwood exam to come to his tiny office. Once the seven of us had squeezed ourselves in, Mr. Harker announced, from a distance of roughly six inches, that we'd passed. All of us.

Our first response was a mere collective "Blimey." (Otherwise speechless, I had to admit that success had a certain allure.) A split-second later, David squealed like a piccolo. The rest of us followed suit, only to be silenced immediately and informed that there was a second element to the selection process, an "interview," to be undergone the Saturday after next.

Every misgiving produced by my first trip to Brentwood resurfaced.

THE SO-CALLED FRIENDLY CHAT with two masters—one of whom had the face of a marmoset, wore a pince-nez, and said nothing during the interview but confined himself instead to reading and rereading several sheets of foolscap covered in what I recognized as my own handwriting, complete with crossings-out and run-amok smudges—still confounds me as an exercise in fine-tuned condescension.

"Do you like sports?" groaned the mute's accomplice, whose snow-white whiskers, staggering obesity, and rumpled gray suit now remind me of nothing so much as a walrus on its deathbed.

"Er . . . sometimes," I said, not quite sure where the question was leading.

"Anything in particular?"

"Er . . . soccer." I immediately wondered whether I might have done better by referring to rugby or cricket.

"I see. And which position do you play?"

"Oh . . . any position really—I really don't mind where they put me," I warbled, only to suspect that he might see this as a symptom of habitual indecision. (Which is not to suggest that such a supposition would have been entirely incorrect.)

"I see. Cricket?"

"We don't play it a lot, sir. And we only play with tennis balls. But I do like rounders. And running."

"I see," he said with a frown. "And . . . ummm . . . what have you been reading lately?"

"Oh, lots of things," I said somewhat diffidently, now painfully aware that mentioning the tennis balls had undoubtedly been a mistake. "I like the Narnia books. And Rosemary Sutcliff and Hilda Lewis. And *Stig of the Dump*. That was good."

"Hmmm. I confiscated that from a new boy just last week. Blighter was reading it in Latin class. You wouldn't do anything like that, would you?"

"Er . . . no."

"Would you like to learn Latin?"

"Er—I think so," I said. "My teacher says I ought to. She knows Latin *and* Greek."

"Really?" he replied, looking lethally unimpressed. "Read any Dickens?"

"Er . . . no," I coughed, now wishing I'd read more than five pages of *Oliver Twist* before putting it aside to be replaced by the Victor Gollancz edition of Robert A. Heinlein's *Orphans of the Sky*.

"Shakespeare?"

"Er . . . not really. But I have read Charles and Mary Lamb. And I liked the film of *Henry V.* With Laurence Oliver."

"It's Olivier, actually. There's an 'i' before the 'e.' "

"Oh," I sniffed, sensing defeat and feeling emotionally winded.

"Well, I wouldn't get too upset about it. You'd better run along now. It's been nice talking to you."

TWO WEEKS LATER, having been rejected by Brentwood, I boarded a bus for Chelmsford, the county town (or capital) of Essex, with my still visibly disappointed mum. I was to interview (without undergoing trial by blots in advance) at a school whose requirements, I could only assume, were less rigorous than Brentwood's even though it had been chartered in 1551.

I took disinterested notice of the vista that opened up when we walked through the gates of King Edward VI Grammar School (referred to as KEGS by the thousands of ticks and vipers who have, if only in the physical sense, survived it), pausing for a moment when I caught sight of the crest, complete with Latin motto, mounted above the plate-glass doors that opened onto the corridor that led to the headmaster's stronghold.

A lantern-jawed secretary led us into his presence and shut the door behind her with a bang that made me jump like a startled hare. It had no effect on the headmaster, a tweed-wrapped middle-aged man with hair *en brosse* and horn-rimmed glasses. He stared at us for several seconds before inviting us to sit down. To my relief, my interview with Nicholas Featherstone, M.A.—an accomplished mathemati-

cian who had once taught at Eton and had an accent that Mum
(she disapproved) thought "fruity"—was pleasantly unfo-
cused and, more to the point, successful.

I SPENT A GOOD DEAL of the following summer trying to
come to terms with the fact—the knowledge alone brought
premature desolation—that the Ramsays, the Burgesses, the
Allports, and Jennifer Walsh would all be leaving Ongar for
good before it was over. David's parents were getting di-
vorced, and Auntie Julia had custody. Edward had been offered a better-paying job lecturing at a teacher-training
college in Yorkshire. Mr. Burgess and Jane had decided to
move (for Matthew's benefit) to a part of London that boasted
what some considered the foremost comprehensive (non-
streamed) school in the country. And Auntie Jennifer had decided, on a whim, to defect to the north coast of Devon. I
would therefore be saying good-bye not just to some of my
most cherished friends but also to five sophisticated adults
whose brains I had always been welcome to pick and whose
books I had always been welcome to read.

My (usually unannounced) visits, my permitted invasions
of a privacy they so generously seemed not to care about,
now took on the taint of desperation. And I became more in-
tensely willing than ever to struggle with varieties of literature that I instinctively knew were beyond me and would
almost certainly remain so for many years to come.

AS THE DAYS PASSED, I also began to inspect more closely (and
ever more fearfully) the sartorial accoutrements of my im-

pending elevation to the fair-to-middling ranks of the cogno-
scenti: blazer, cap, regulation raincoat, short gray trousers,
sensible shoes, and crest-emblazoned tie. I also routinely
(meaning morning, noon, and night) stuffed my brand-new
satchel, which was roughly the size of my torso, as full of
books as possible, slung it over my skeletal shoulder with the
strap at the shortest setting, and then, blindly ignoring all
creeping things (primarily slugs and snails) that chose to
cross my maddened path, circled the garden several dozen
times, trying to prove to myself that I was physically capable
of bearing such a load from home to bus stop and from bus
station to school.

Dad thought the entire performance ridiculous, which, of
course, it was, but was kind enough to allow me to persist in it
when his first attempt at discouragement initialed a sortie of
wailing. Snails and their less protected cousins continued to
die messy deaths by the dozen, squeezed to decease in mind-
less droves and coating the soles of my shoes with a mucilagi-
nous grit (mixed with bruised grass and a caking of mud) in
whose removal with a rusty paint scraper I was completely
absorbed—watched by a curious Joy, who was vacantly suck-
ing on a Kit Kat—one windy Sunday afternoon when Mr.
Burgess dropped by and announced that he and Jane and
Matthew would soon be leaving for a camping holiday in
France and would love to take me with them.

Mum, transfigured in an instant by an unusually broad and
(I thought) suspiciously greedy wreath of smiles, immediately pranced on air for five exultant minutes, then scampered
upstairs, with muffled thuds engendered by a recently purchased nylon carpet the color of cut-price mustard, to tap her
supine husband on his unprotected neck and inform him of

what she suspected might just be a once-in-a-lifetime opportunity for his son. Dad, who knew very well by now that any
failure to defer to Mum's opinion on the subject of my
prospects and attainments would compromise the quiet life he
longed for, agreed on the spot and went back to sleep.

A few minutes after Mr. Burgess had taken one last dubi-
ous look at the scandalous state of my shoes and left, Joy, to
whom I had, as always, been paying no attention at all, ran up
to Mum, who was now attaching a hundredweight of washing
to our clothesline.

"I want to go to France, too," she said, her circular face a
marsh of milk chocolate and tears. "Why can't I go? Why
didn't Mr. Burgess and Jane invite me?"

"Because you're too little," said Mum.

"Dorothy Dixon went to France last year," Joy sputtered.
"And she's only seven." (Dorothy was the sister of Derek
Dixon, who was one of my friends; Joy was now nine.)

"I know that," said Mum. "And I bet she didn't learn a
thing—but John will."

At this, Joy's unsullied skin, from Start-rite shoes to pink
barrette, turned several shades of purple. Next, she seemed to
shrivel and age before my startled eyes. Her head collapsed to
a shrunken crunch of umbrage, her blouse became a postage
stamp, her knockabout skirt a muffin cup, her cardigan merely
a whisper of the wool from which it had been knitted by
Jackie. And then she returned to her normal height, her normal weight, and exploded.

"Why's it always John?" she yelled. "Why's it always
John? It's not fair. Why? Why? Why?"

Her final "Why?" protracted into weeping, which made
me decidedly uncomfortable but, given how frequently she

and I scrapped, complete with kicks and fisticuffs (I always won), failed to spark my sympathy.

"That's enough of that, my girl," barked Mum, dropping one of Dad's Van Heusen shirts, which came to rest in a corner of the flower bed where Twinkle had recently relieved himself, via the rear sluice, at indigestible length.

"Why can't I go to France, too? Why can't I have a nice holiday?" Joy suddenly screamed so loudly that Auntie Jennifer deserted her deck chair and stuck her head over the fence to ask what on earth was the matter.

Mum was now looking upset for the simple reason that her daughter's question had queried the diet, a distant cry from Bournemouth's overfeeding, on which we'd subsisted, to my distress as well, during the previous year's vacation, in Cornwall: toast at first light, a ham sandwich for dinner, another ham sandwich for tea, all of it consumed in what I deprecated as "that grubby little hut near Truro."

I continued to scrape away at flattened gastropods. Mum went indoors. Auntie Jennifer took Joy for a walk that lasted an hour and yielded enough blackberries for half a dozen jars of viscous jam.

CHAPTER 6

The Hasty Consumption of Pilchards

· · · ·

EIGHT DAYS LATER, AT SEVEN IN THE MORNING, A FERRY
named the *Dragon,* bound for Le Havre and packed with
smarter cars than Dad's and several hundred, as I supposed,
studious people, slipped her moorings and slowly, calmly,
nosed her way across the shining surface of the Solent. Moments later, the Burgess expedition went belowdecks for breakfast, which turned out to be a cheerless affair staged in a space
so painfully overlit that some of the more sensitive passengers
wore sunglasses. There, I swiftly demolished a heaping plate of
stone-cold button mushrooms, lukewarm tomatoes, overcooked bacon, generic baked beans, runny fried eggs, barely
off-white toast, and underpricked bangers whose sawdust small
intestines were spurting from the untreatable wounds in their
skin.

My companions, on the other hand, hardly touched their
food, and Mr. Burgess was complaining, loudly enough to be
audible in the engine room, about having been compelled to

pay far too much money for a "load of bloody rubbish." That many of the other passengers expressed agreement did something to soothe him, as did Matthew's diplomatic suggestion that a nicer *repas* could probably be had for just a few francs once we were ashore. It was only at this juncture that all three of them noticed that I had disposed of a meal they considered inedible.

I immediately felt not only both stupid and embarrassed but glumly aware, despite the kindness they had always shown me, of the existence of a chasm between us, an abyss that I could never hope to bridge even if I passed every exam I had yet to take—which I knew very well was unlikely.

A FEW MINUTES LATER, I was enthroned on a bench at the *Dragon*'s bow, distractedly trying with one hand to tweezer carbonized sausage skin and scraps of bacon rind from between my two front teeth and, with the other, to scrawl, in a sixpenny spiral-bound notepad, the very first lines of the written record of my travels that Mum had insisted I make on pain of cessation of pocket money. I was interrupted by the sight of two gray-painted jets hurtling toward us.

"Navy Buccaneers, I think," I yelped, jubilantly stunned by their shock wave and howl and watching in amazement as the hundreds of gulls wheeling in our wake lurched to starboard in a collective convulsion of terror and the aircraft themselves made a super-tight turn to the north with no deviation that I could see in the distance between their wingtips and the waves.

"Right first time," said Mr. Burgess. "I didn't know you liked planes, John."

"My auntie gave me a book about planes and some Airfix models for Christmas," I said flatly, none too sure that "liked" was, as yet, quite the mot juste and suddenly remembering that Jackie considered the Burgesses very nice people but somewhat "upper," their accents a bit too "cut-glass" for her comfort, despite the fact that her married boyfriend (an import-export broker who happened to be her boss and who also, several years later, offered to "pull a few strings" to help me get a short-service commission in the Army) was much more upper and much better-off.

"Bloody good plane, the Buccaneer," said Mr. Burgess, who probably knew that one of its missions in the event of hostilities would be to lob nuclear bombs onto any Soviet battle group bound for the North Atlantic. "Noisy bugger, too."

"You're not kidding," I grinned.

"Did you see those missiles glued to their wings? Monsters. Must make a hell of a bang."

"I bet they do," I said. (It occurs to me now, however, that the "missiles" may have been drop tanks.)

The breeze began to stiffen, a middle-aged lady with a dystrophic smile buzzed by us in a self-propelled wheelchair, and a herd of older boys in smart school uniforms stood beneath one of the lifeboats and sang a preposterous song about saying good-bye to a horse.

"Did you know what those planes were, Matthew?" asked Jane, without looking up from Gore Vidal's *Messiah*.

"No," said Matthew, in a tone suggesting that he considered the question completely beneath his dignity. "I didn't. Does it matter?"

"Yes it bloody does," snapped Mr. Burgess, who still attended an occasional Dartmouth reunion and would probably

have achieved flag rank by now had he chosen to stay in the
Navy after the war. "What the hell do you think a Buccaneer's
for, boy? Air shows only? Princess Anne's christening? The
Queen's bloody birthday? Flypasts and bugger-all else?"

"Of course not. They're supposed to stop the Russians."

"Exactly. Blow the buggers out of the water before they
know what's hit them."

"Could they?"

"Probably not," said Mr. Burgess. "Rumor has it we're
hopelessly outnumbered."

THE NICER *REPAS* (which, Matthew reminded me, was known
as *petit déjeuner*) was procured for what Mr. Burgess called
"next to *rien*" at eight the following morning in a workmen's
café in Giverny. It came in the form of croissants and what
looked and felt like a gallon of cocoa, served up in vessels that
took a lot of lifting and, being neither cup nor bowl, were
therefore presumably prime examples of what Dad had meant
by "basins" when discoursing on orphanage breakfasts. (The
adults drank café au lait.) I found the cocoa rich but mildly
bitter, an unfamiliar but far from unpleasant combination that
I thought worth recording.

I did not, however, make mention of the exhibition unfurling across the street, where several elderly Frenchmen wearing grimy berets and raincoats were sitting on a bench outside
a bar and swigging red wine from the bottle. I also decided
that it might be an idea not to inform my family that I had dug
and made use of my first latrine the previous evening while
camping in the middle of nowhere, which was Mr. Burgess's
locale of choice for parking the Volkswagen Traveler, erect-

ing the tents, and reading a few more pages of *Madame Bo-vary* by the primrose flicker of a hurricane lamp while Jane made tinned-tuna stew.

Next, Mr. Burgess unfolded a map and announced that we were going to spend a few hours—with recessional for picnicking—in and around one of the most beautiful churches on the face of the earth. As a result, I shuffled into Chartres Cathedral two hours later with my mind set on food, not religion, and hungrily took no notable note of my surrounds until we were more than halfway down the nave, at which point Mr. Burgess turned me about and told me to look up.

The torrent of stained glass that greeted my eyes left me subdued for the rest of the day, for it suggested a kind of inspiration I couldn't even begin to get to grips with. (Not until I read André Malraux's *The Voices of Silence* several years later would I begin to have a glimmer of understanding about what it was that I'd witnessed.) That night, while digging my second latrine, I reminded myself that camping didn't suit me.

MY JOURNAL ENTRIES became increasingly sporadic as our travels continued, largely because Mr. Burgess had devised an itinerary so ambitious that I was usually tuckered out by the time our daily tuna had been consumed and Matthew and I had made a predictably ineffectual job of washing the dishes in a pint of tepid water while Jane, who had finished *Messiah*, made minuscule notes in the margins of a water-damaged copy of *Light in August*.

Our circumnavigation of a considerable portion of France took us first along the Loire Valley (where we walked what seemed like miles inside the most influential châteaux) via Vendôme (where Matthew and I were lightly beaten up by half a dozen contrarian adolescents from a children's home in Paris and I first enjoyed crêpes Suzette), Angers (where Matthew and I spent a blisteringly hot afternoon at a municipal swimming pool and got sunburned), Montreuil-Bellay (where Matthew and I were allowed half a glass of Vouvray each with our noontide cheese and subsequently had trouble staying awake during a tour of the Chapelle St.-Jean), and Ancenis, where Mr. Burgess, having booked us into a pension with paper-thin walls and chilly bidets, declaimed his intention to take us all out to dinner.

THE MAIN THING that struck me as we were escorted, far from ceremoniously, to our table by a diminutive maître d' who was sporting a proboscis as intrusive as General de Gaulle's was the intense concentration with which the other diners were applying themselves to their food.

Mr. Burgess naturally took charge of the ordering, assessing the menu at considerable length and, whenever confronted with an unfamiliar term, referring to Larousse. This practice had the unfortunate (and understandable) effect of making our waiter feel so redundant that the automatic indifference with which he had initially greeted us rapidly devolved into a virtuoso demonstration of Gallic superciliousness.

That snails were apparently edible came as a shock whose force was swiftly blunted by the flavor of the sauce in which they were swimming, and I wasted no time in disposing of both with the aid of a fork (which I thought effete) and a basket of bread. Matthew seemed less impressed, which surprised me, for even though I had yet to encounter the term "cosmopolitan tastes," I was, somewhere in the depths of my unconscious, already certain he had them.

Shortly before the *truite au bleu* arrived, Mr. Burgess gave the wine list a once-over and eventually alighted on Sancerre while sipping, at Jane's reprimand, on a prophylactic coffee. (He'd already had two Pernods.) I found the trout's flesh too coarse (and almost gamy) for my taste but mopped up every drop of the hollandaise sauce, which Mr. Burgess accused of being about to break, with yet another *panier de pain*. The Sancerre, however, had much the same effect on me—in terms of triggering yet another dependency—as Mr. Pitt's supremely aphotic coffee. Matthew, however, would have much preferred Vouvray.

"This stuff tastes like grass," he choked.

"Bloody good job, too," said Mr. Burgess. "If it didn't, I'd send it back."

"I preferred the wine we had in Montreuil."

"Hmmm," muttered Mr. Burgess. "I'm not so sure about that stuff anymore. Chap at the office recommended it. Bit of a sissy wine, if you ask me. Tasted like a bunch of bloody flowers."

For dessert, we had a chocolate mousse even richer than the single scoop each of handmade ice cream—an exceptionally welcome intermission from incessantly sun-slimed ham sandwiches—that Joy and I had been allowed on our last day in Cornwall, the day before Dad drove us home from dawn to dusk, three hundred miles in fifteen hours, with just enough money for petrol and not so much as a sixpence, jolly or otherwise, for anything to eat. The journey thus included my first experience of something uncomfortably close to genuine hunger, which left me perplexed, ashamed, and secretly angry for several weeks.

The second incarnation of afters, over which we lingered until the restaurant's only occupants were the Burgess excursion, a couple who couldn't stop smiling at each other, and a pensive quartet of impeccably dressed businessmen, was cheese, accompanied by still more Sancerre (half a glass, in my case, from the evening's second bottle, and no glass, no thank you, in Matthew's).

At what felt like midnight but in backwater Ancenis almost certainly wasn't, the maître d', minus his tie, walked over with the *addition* (a logical word, said Matthew, when you stop to think about it) and presented it to Mr. Burgess, who extracted a fistful of francs from his wallet and told Jane that he hadn't had so much fun since the monumental booze-up with which he and his fellow diving instructors had marked the occasion of Germany's unconditional surrender.

BACK AT THE PENSION, into which we were followed by the entrepreneurs and the lovebirds, Matthew and I inserted a sufficient quantity of sous into a vending machine to persuade it to disgorge two ice-cold Cokes and went to our room, a few doors down a dim corridor from Mr. Burgess's and Jane's.

Cokes dispatched with myriad burps, we crawled into our beds, which had crevassed mattresses, only to sit bolt upright a few minutes later. Sounds I couldn't place—a kind of laughter, with something about it of children in hysterics at the sight of Mickey Mouse and Donald Duck, a kind of thudding that brought to mind the thump-thump-thump of the *Dragon*'s propellers, and something a lot like crying but with none of

Joy's inconsolability—were coming through the wall from the room next door.

"Oh dear," murmured Matthew. "I think I know what's happening."

"What?"

His explanation, as anatomically exhaustive as might have been expected from a future lecturer in biology at Cambridge, appalled me, differing as it did in almost every detail not only from the inaccuracies I'd managed to pick up at school but also from the well-scrubbed platitudes contained in the book *Susie's Babies* (Susie was a hamster), which Mum had assured me would put something called "the facts of life" in perspective.

THE *DEUXIÈME* AND *TROISIÈME SEMAINES* of our twenty-one-day trip took us through Brittany and Normandy via Carnac (where a fall from a dolmen left me with a twisted ankle and a direct order from Mr. Burgess to "bloody well stop climbing things"), Concarneau (where we lunched on what Mr. Burgess thought a too-oily, as in "over-sardined," but "still decent" *cotriade*), Douarnenez (where the Traveler's captain roused us at a godless hour for a trip to a fish auction), Bayeux, and the Côte de Nacre. Our last port of call was Honfleur (the birthplace, Jane said, of Satie), where we stayed for one more day than we'd intended because Mr. Burgess came down with jaundice, which entailed a string of frantic phone calls to the ferry company and a "sobering visit," said Mr. Burgess, to an unsympathetic doctor.

We spent the extra day snacking on cheese with our noses in books on the fusty banks of a man-made lake—a shadow,

Jane imagined, of its nineteenth-century glory—that anchored the demesne, now inexpensive campground, of an impoverished vicomte. This nobleman would fry a runny egg
for every human, great or small, who cared to visit the kitchen
(a lot like Eleanor Ramsay's) where he spent the widowed
plupart of his time.

Mr. Burgess, at Jane's suggestion, was now reading *Brides-
head Revisited* (whose author's name I had mispronounced, to
Matthew's amusement, as "Wawg"), Jane had begun *Go Tell It
on the Mountain*, Matthew (who had just finished Asimov's
Foundation and Empire) was playing a third game of chess with
himself, and I was engrossed in chapter one of *The Spy Who
Came in from the Cold*.

"Good man, Waugh, you know, Janie," said Mr. Burgess.
"I've heard he once took Greene to task for all that bloody
adultery. Damn good on character as well. Julia's put-down
of Rex—remember that?"

"Not verbatim, darling."

" 'It's just that he isn't a real person at all; he's just a few
faculties of a man highly developed.' Bit grim, eh?"

"I suppose he must have known someone just like it."

"Don't we all?"

"I don't think I do."

"What about—?"

"Please don't name names, dear."

"It's such fun to name names."

"No, it's not," said Jane, irritably.

"It's quite the avocation in the Navy, I can tell you. If a
chap's no bloody good, he soon gets to hear about it."

"Yes, well, you aren't in the Navy anymore, darling.
You've been out for twenty years."

"Mr. Burgess," I interrupted, waving Le Carré and feeling impelled, as I often did in the Burgesses' company and always without success, to sound intelligent. "The bit about being a bit of a man. There's something like it here . . . somewhere . . . about Leamas . . . 'A man who was not quite a gentleman.' "

"Oh yes," said Mr. Burgess. "I remember that. Strange thing."

He fell silent.

"Strange thing, Mr. Burgess?" I asked.

"The gentleman business."

"My mum says you're one—and an officer. I mean. In the war."

Jane twitched.

"Nice girl, your mum," said Mr. Burgess. "Bit batty at times, mind you."

"For God's sake, Julian," snapped Jane.

"Oh, come on, old girl." He grinned. "I've had a joke or two about Kitty with John before. Anyway. We're a nation of bloody eccentrics. It's nothing to be ashamed of. Very single-minded woman, she is. The way she keeps John and Joy up to the mark. She wants the best for both of you. Isn't that right, John?"

"Er—yes."

"And," Mr. Burgess continued, "she does rather tend—in my opinion—to take, well, a rose-tinted view of people she sees as, hmmm, the educated sort. Must be under the illusion that there's an element of perfection in there somewhere. And by the way, John, if anyone's a gentleman, your dad is."

"That's true," said Matthew. I immediately forgave him for the lecture on reproduction, although I still couldn't bring myself to award a moment's credence to his indelicate information that some people considered oysters—I'd spat one out in public view during a pit stop in Cancale—an aphrodisiac.

"And," said Mr. Burgess, "they'll probably feed you a bloody great load of balls about being a gentleman. At that grammar school you're going to. Take my advice, take all that with a big pinch of salt. I'll tell you how to make yourself useful: keep your nose clean, do your best, women and children first."

This observation, though well meant, did nothing to calm my nerves.

UPON MY RETURN, Mum was less than pleased to discover that my journal ran to a mere four paragraphs of almost illegible gibberish supplemented by several dozen postcards. I incurred her displeasure again a week later, when she upbraided me for having continued to spend a huge proportion of my leisure time reading *Victor* and *Valiant* despite my continuing exposure, thanks to Edward and Mr. Burgess, to a measure of serious writing (Siegfried Sassoon, Wilfred Owen, Edmund Blunden, Henri Barbusse, and Keith Douglas) about the wars.

Bored with the Beatles and nursing a stomachache caused by the hasty consumption of pilchards, I was holed up in the living room and squinting at a hardback I had borrowed from Edward on the strength of its title when Mum interrupted.

"What's wrong with you?" she squawked. "Get up and switch the light on right now. And you can pick up all those comics while you're at it, or they're damn well going in the dustbin. I don't know why you read those things—your dad and me are spending a fortune on books for you and Joy. Or hadn't you noticed?"

"Of course I have."

"I'm glad to hear it."

She stopped and restarted.

"What's this one, then?"

"What's what one?"

"The book."

"Oh. It's called *The Swordbearers*. Borrowed it from Edward."

"So what's it about?"

"The First World War. The men in charge. Ludendorff. Jellicoe. That lot."

"Oh, yes. The men in charge. Of one almighty balls-up after another. Hardly your grandpa's favorite people."

More silence.

"Still, at least it's a book. I do wish you'd stop reading comics. I'm not going to tell you *not* to read them. You'll have to make your own mind up. One of these days. But isn't it time you grew out of them? They're a mockery. Ever seen a bloke with both legs missing in *Valiant?* Or a chap with half his face blown off in *Victor?*"

"No."

"Or how about a man with no head?" she said, in a tone of voice that particularly upset me, combining as it did something that felt like self-pity with a rage that I suddenly realized might not be directed at me. "Your grandpa saw that."

LATER THAT EVENING, Phil Skipton, resplendent in his habitual baggy overcoat and antiquated trilby, knocked at our front door.

"This is for you," he said, proffering a Scotch-taped paper

bag. Having hefted the package for weight and wondered whether it might not be a half-pound bar of chocolate, I tore it open and found myself confronting a copy of *Roget's Thesaurus,* a Penguin for which Phil had paid six shillings. Reading the inscription was enough to persuade me that my days as a member of the Puffin Club were perhaps irremediably numbered:

> To John on becoming a "Grammar School Boy." At first you may wonder what this book is all about—but open it anywhere every day and read it for two minutes and you will find it full of treasure. Before you are 21 we hope it will be falling to pieces and you will be asking for a bigger and better one. With love from the Skiptons.

A follow-up glance at the volume's interior put their annihilation beyond all doubt. Having thanked Phil for the gift—which I still possess—I trudged upstairs to my bedroom and pushed the latest entrant to my library into a gap between *Journey to the Center of the Earth* and *Tarka the Otter.*

CHAPTER 7

Cocoa and Corned Beef Sandwiches

. . . .

ON THE MORNING OF SEPTEMBER 10, 1965, MY FIRST DAY AT
KEGS, I got up far too early and traipsed downstairs in full
regalia to find Dad preparing to depart for a day shift. He
poured me some tea and made me a bacon sandwich. Once he
had left, I went into the dining room, opened a window an
inch or so, and sat in part darkness while, down at the end of
the garden, a shambles of hawthorn broke into song, the
anisette peeps of a robin or two unevenly competing with the
ack-tattle-tat of the starlings.

Gone for good were the six long years that had rubbed my
rarely shining face in minatory math, Palgrave's poetry, met-
ric tons of Polly-Wog (a pasty glue that stuck nothing to
nothing securely and took several hours to dry), kilometers of
Plasticine, carefree hours of semicompetitive sportsmanship,
and the sheer impossibility (in my case) of turning several
yards of raffia into a mat that a mother might deign to position
beneath a fruit bowl.

At a quarter to eight, I tugged on my raincoat, shouldered my satchel, quietly closed the front door behind me, and walked down Mayflower Way to the bus stop near the station, minus Mum's glare of concern (she wasn't feeling well) and musing in disorder on Bayeux, Buccaneers, and *The Hawk in the Rain*; on privies in Limehouse, on Dick and a disappeared legion of sergeants drinking like fish in Bombay; on what the Grand Fleet had for tea (cocoa and corned beef sandwiches) during a break in the Battle of Jutland, on the removal of Grandpa's best friend's head by a whizz-bang in 1916.

Forty-five minutes later, my friend Terry Taylor (whose parents were Cockneys) and I, caps on our heads and our socks at half-mast, were in Chelmsford, slogging our way along Broomfield Road in an autumnal drizzle the color of unwashed sheep.

"Tell you what," he huffed, then puffed, as the gates of KEGS came looming into view. "I'm fucking fed up already."

"Me and all," I stammered in rising panic.

With mental fingers firmly crossed and short pants neatly creased, we careered through the gates and were quickly ensnared by an angular man with a dog collar snagged on his wattles.

"You're almost," he murmured, "abysmally late."

"I'm sorry, sir, I really am," I said.

"Your names?"

"Haney."

"Haney? Ah . . . John Haney. You, boy, will be in 1A."

"Taylor," said Terry.

"Taylor, Terence? 1C, my lad."

"Norton," wailed a wan macaque who had slunk up behind us with his cap on backward, his skinny arms barely containing a ripped, mephitic duffel bag that now began to regurgitate a bottle of Quink, a pair of dividers, a pencil case, a Wagon Wheel, a protractor, a bag of barley twists, and a pornographic magazine.

"Tut-tut-tut, Norton," the clergyman sniffed, attempting to ram *Penthouse* into his overcoat pocket without slackening his grip on either his umbrella or his long list of minors. Finally, having succeeded by means of contortions that made him resemble a stick insect having a panic attack, the Reverend William Wilkinson-Fuller (classics taught full-time, ethics incessantly) dispersed us to our respective herds, all three of which were shivering deep in the shade of a molting elm.

A FEW MINUTES LATER—by which time I'd noticed that among the new boys were several I recognized from my trips to Brentwood—Mr. Featherstone flung open the doors that barred the approach to his sanctum and sauntered toward us, impeccably dressed in what I now think of as a London Wall overcoat, Bishopsgate shoes, Cannon Street pants, and a Pimlico trilby. In his stately backwash bobbed three mortals of lesser degree.

The first, Mr. Jackson (Jake, to the inmates), taught history and would, he declared, be keeping 1C as pinned down as possible until overrun or relieved. (Fate had smeared Jake with a globular body, a spherical head, and a pallor that matched the Mantuan's in Dante.)

The second, Mr. D. G. Lane (Bronco, as in the television cowpoke Bronco Layne), taught classics and intended, by his own admission, to make 1B the best class in its year. (David Lane was a dragonfly's tail from his slender neck down and a patchy terrazzo of five o'clock shadow and Coke-bottle glasses above it.)

The third, Mr. Kettle (Larry, born Lawrence), who'd been saddled with 1A, wrestled with numbers both Pythagorean (quadratic, unequal, confusing, reductive) and less so (Venn diagrams, subsets, and vectors), none of which would ever make sense to me despite long hours of desperate coaching by Dad.

1A, 1B, and 1C were next repelled across a muddy football pitch to Westfields, a two-story building, clad in underfed ivy, that reminded me of daguerrotypes of Gladstone in his dotage. 1C snaked into a room on the ground floor while 1A and 1B clattered up a gloomy flight of insupportable stairs. Once we were seated at our desks and had made what we could of the legends knifed into their lids—WOT NO TEA?, DO YOU LIKE IT UP THE ARSE?, WE WON THE WAR, and FUCK OFF— Mr. Kettle directed our attention to the printed matter piled amid the obscenities: first-year Latin, ancient history (early attempts at cultivation; Cleopatra's asp), English as a mere technicality (the life cycle of the pronoun), the selfsame tongue in full narrative spate (a Victorian novel, now justly forgotten, *The Cloister and the Hearth*), a pamphlet on geography (the output per country of pig iron, sisal, and coal), and a young person's guide to biology (pinnate leaves; odontoid pegs; sacrums; saliva).

At 12:15, we went to lunch, which was quickly consumed, eight boys to a tumbledown trestle, in the refectory (something like the biscuit tin but bigger) and consisted of liver, potatoes, and peas, roughed up by packet-mix gravy. This dish was followed by a two-part "afters" that was shortly to prove my undoing: chocolate sponge pudding and chocolate custard, which limped from the jug like porridge. Four of my seven companions, disgusted by the main course, had no interest in its successor, which I therefore began to divide among the gluttons, a procedure promptly arrested by Mr. Benson, the master on lunch patrol. Twisting my left ear— the pain led to panic, immobilized eyes, and shortness of breath—and bellowing into the other from a distance of a centimeter, he informed me that I had earned myself an addition to the coming weekend's homework: writing out, two hundred times, "It is most important that food be shared equally at the school lunch table."

A QUARTER OF AN HOUR LATER, Terry and I and three other new boys, including Nigel Norton, were waylaid in transition back to Westfields by a marauding flotilla of exceptionally shabby fifth formers whose subsequent demonstration of apparently permissible derangement made it plain why none of them would ever wear the nicely cut blazer and stylish black tie, with understated green and silver stripes, that proclaimed the august presence of a prefect.

Having first addressed us, while doling out an avalanche of prefatory blows to chest, solar plexus, and stomach, as "ticks," "bugs," "turds," "an absolute shower" (a vilification much used in the Army), "a horrible sight" (the armed forces again), "spastics," "mongs" (a common slur, at better schools, on mental retardation), and, finally, "cunts" (which, despite my perpetual deployment of "fuck," still had the power to shock me), they threw us into a holly bush that I would probably have classified, under more auspicious circumstances, as a quite majestic instance of the species.

This substantiation of my insignificance naturally did nothing to reconcile me to the fact that the emancipatory hour of four o'clock was still four interminable (forty-five-minute) "periods" away; looming in my future were an hour and a half of a "modern language" and the same extent of an as yet undisclosed "sport." Barely managing not to whimper and already wondering why a better class of secondary education had—apparently with some regularity—to hurt like hell, I bandaged my bleeding knees with two of the half dozen British Home Stores handkerchiefs that Jackie and Grandpa had given me—along with *Moonfleet, Johnny Tremain,* and *The Observer's Book of Aircraft*—the previous Christmas.

THE AFTERNOON HALF of my first day at KEGS opened with what turned out to be a welcome stretch of French, which was taught by Alice (Ma) Smith, an even-tempered woman in her fifties and the only teacher in the entire school who never raised her voice and never said an unkind word. "Buffoon," "dolt," "dunce," "idiot," and, even worse, "cretin" were otherwise pandemic and quickly unnerved me so badly that I developed a tic consisting of an absolute inability to get out a word unless I first prefaced it with a cascade of peculiar clicking sounds. Which is how it came about that between the ages of eleven and thirteen—when the affliction unaccountably vanished overnight—I was referred to by my classmates as the Tick-Tock Man.

The second half of the afternoon was devoted to soccer, which I would probably have enjoyed had the master in charge, a cantankerous ridgeback named Sturridge, been less indifferent to a succession of fouls that eventually resulted in two sprained ankles, a badly cracked shin, and, in my case, an unjustified kick in each knee—I was nowhere near the ball at the time—that not only necessitated further use of one of Jackie's handkerchiefs but also elicited a much-needed effusion of sympathy from Mum, who, beholding the dismal sight I presented upon returning to No. 13, not only made me an enormous helping of baked beans on toast but allowed me to read the *Beezer* while shoveling it down.

The rest of the week went more smoothly. By the time the bell rang (at three fifty-five on the Featherstone dot) that Friday, I'd handed my lines to Mr. Benson, made several new friends, learned not to quake when compelled to shower with everyone else in 1A, and, despite a not-infrequent ache in my twice-mistreated knees, fallen in love with cross-country running, a sport that involved neither kicking nor gouging and allowed me twenty minutes or so of fleshly solitude and a respite from having to try to adjust to a place where I already knew for certain I stood no chance of feeling at home.

TWO DAYS LATER, a telephone call from an agitated Jackie corrupted the quasi-Cistercian (and, in the wake of another parental fracas the previous evening, much appreciated) serenity that had engulfed us shortly after Sunday dinner. I had my nose in *The Thirty-nine Steps*, Joy was engrossed in *Worzel Gummidge*, Mum was reading *The Thin Red Line*, and Dad was submersed in a technical manual.

Grandpa, said Jackie, had fallen from a ladder while fixing

a gutter and was now prostrate in the hospital with a broken leg, a fractured arm, a bandaged head, severe concussion, and a measure of fame as a "tough old boot" for having survived a fall that could, it appeared, have killed him. Dad dashed outside to start the car (which, to Mum's dudgeon, took almost twenty minutes), and the Skiptons looked after Joy and me for the rest of the day, spoiling us with sloppily scrambled eggs ad infinitum, bottomless pots of Ty-Phoo tea, all the aniseed balls we wanted, and a virtual masque of mantic recitations from Shakespeare and Sitwell and Hardy.

Grandpa returned home three weeks later and remained an invalid until his death in 1968—an incontinent, semi-demented wraith confined to a cot in a downstairs room and cared for by Jackie. When not at the office, she fed him, watered him, washed him, and gave him his medicine. And during the three years it took him to die, Joy and I were not allowed (to spare our feelings and his, we supposed) to see him. Our haunted hero thus became, quite literally, the skeleton in what was left of the Bush-related cupboard.

BY 1967, Dad was working sixty hours a week and Mum was putting in forty and finding time as well, on non-Redbridge weekends, for the perpetual advancement of her culture campaign. This involved trips to the theater, to galleries, and to the cinema, where Joy and I not only watched run-of-the-mill fare (*The Big Country, Dumbo, In Search of the Castaways, How the West Was Won,* and *Mary Poppins*) but were also made to grapple, now and then, with farragoes more mind-dilating. We tore through our ice cream and plastic-trapped peanuts while gaping (on occasion in London's West End) at distractions I suspected would not have been viewed on the Isle of Dogs as a profitable alternative to a packet of crisps and a beer: *Citizen Kane*, Tati's *Les Vacances de Monsieur Hulot*, and Cocteau's *La Belle et la bête*. This last was less of an infliction for Joy, who couldn't follow the subtitles, than might have been expected, since she'd persevered with art (even though it counted for nothing at Top School) and knew a transcendent image when she saw one.

Despite Mum's best efforts, however, neither the culture campaign nor the three years I spent in the Boys' Brigade, an organization for putatively devout Christian youths between the ages of eleven and eighteen, proved capable of disconnecting, disabling, defusing, or even slightly reducing my interest—all comics, by now, behind me and books to the fore—in the military cosmopolis, in Stalingrad and Crete, in the Maginot Line, Monte Cassino, Verdun, the Ardennes, and Poltava.

She was, therefore, not too dumbfounded when, in the spring of 1968 (I was fourteen), I informed her that I had left the Boys' Brigade and planned to join the recently established Ongar Flight of No. 424 Squadron (West Essex Wing) of the Air Training Corps, to which Simon Stevens (an acquaintance from KEGS) had been admitted a few months earlier. Dad was more supportive (he'd been in the ATC prior to being, as he put it, "press-ganged into the Army") but suspected that I would probably find the bait— a one-week summer camp every year at an operational RAF base, shooting, gliding, a guaranteed minimum of thirty minutes of flying per annum aboard a De Havilland Chipmunk, a piston-engined two-seat primary trainer—an insufficient return on an annual investment of fifty parade nights largely focused on drill.

I refused to be deterred.

IN THOSE DAYS, the ATC was commanded at the squadron and regional levels by civilians commissioned in the RAFVR(T)—the Training Branch of the Royal Air Force Volunteer Reserve—and, at the highest echelons, by serving and retired regular Air Force officers. A primary aim of the organization is to encourage acne-ravaged boys (and nowadays, but not in my time, girls) to contemplate a career in the RAF. This being the case, there was a prodigious aggregation of defecating pimples on display when I arrived at the Ongar Flight drill hut at seven o'clock on my first Friday evening (half an hour before parade officially began) and was immediately awarded a preliminary crash course in standing to attention by a pasty-faced eighteen-year-old cadet warrant officer named Derek (Dolly) Newman.

Dolly was built like a dustbin and had, said Simon, reputedly "done it" with every barmaid under thirty who worked within five miles of the cottage in nearby High Ongar where he lived with his mum and his granny. The two other newest potential recruits that night were Sammy Seal, who lived next door to the young lady who would become my very first not-quite-consummatory girlfriend—Victoria MacKinnon, a Hellenist in vitro, had the most majestic breasts, the widest hips, and the most inflammatory smile I'd ever seen—and Ronnie Dos Santos, a black kid whose parents had been born in Mozambique.

At seven-thirty, Flight Lieutenant Brian Staines, an elderly officer from squadron headquarters in neighboring Debden, whose sobriquet (Sticky) had to do with his sadly clammy handshake, tottered in. He was accompanied by Flight Lieutenant Bertie (Bighead) Stanton (his second-in-command) and a dour-looking, extremely tall civilian instructor named Ivan (Tiny) Rutherford. Tiny, a foreman at a paper mill, was soon to be commissioned as a pilot officer (PO).

Neither Sticky nor Tiny (nor Bighead), who were slowly pursued by Sergeant Walter Bannerman and Corporal Daniel Dawson, seemed pleased with the spectacle upon which they'd stumbled. The other cadets—including Simon, whose head-bisecting grin was at odds with the cheerless mien he invariably presented at school—had taken advantage of Dolly's preoccupation with the probationers by playing a singularly feral game of footer with a hairless tennis ball.

Wally immediately marched over to Dolly, tapped him on his corrugated back, and hissed, "Sticky's here, you stupid fucking bastard." Dolly about-faced in a flash, came to attention with a downburst of the right boot that shook the hut so hard the windowpanes shook in their sashes, gave Sticky a frenzied salute that Sticky chose not to return, and screamed, "Tallest on the right, shortest on the left—flight, fall in— other right, for Christ's sake, other right."

Sammy and Ronnie and I, as ordered, stood at the back and, mortally expectant, stayed mum.

Once the miscreants (most of them habitués of Top School) had fallen in and been inspected ("Next time you try to press that uniform, please remember to plug the iron in first") and condemned ("I need to see a lot more discipline here, a lot more") by Bighead, Sticky went to deal with Dolly (now looking far from cocksure) in the broom closet otherwise known as the flight commander's office. Tiny, for his part, announced that the evening's entertainment would consist of an hour of drill, a shorter (as punishment) tea break than usual, and an hour of aircraft recognition.

The break, a relief to participants and spectators alike, was masterminded by Wally's mother, Edna. This sparrow of a woman in her fifties, when not producing tea and beefburgers for the human equivalent of *vin ordinaire,* mended umbrellas for a gentlemen's clothier in Chelmsford. I liked her immediately.

Halfway through my second urgent burger of the evening, Simon introduced me to Wally, who turned out to be a prospective Dump success to the modest extent that his teachers believed he might just scrape through enough O Levels to go on to do his A's (as in "Advanced"), either at KEGS or at Chelmsford Technical High School. Through Simon, I also met Corporal Joseph Garrett, a towering Aryan blond whose dad was in the stratosphere at Shell.

"Another fucker from KEGS, eh?" grimaced Wally with a twinkle in his eye that made it plain that his apparent distaste wasn't completely sincere.

"Yes," I replied, inclined to grin but not yet ready to risk it. "Anything wrong with that?"

"Maybe not—but we'll see." He ripped open a bag of crisps. "I hope you've got a few more fucking brains than poor old Simon."

"Get fucking stuffed," said Simon, whose house had intrigued me the first time I went there because it contained no reading material other than gray-scale magazines entirely concerned with meticulously overblown motorbikes and (to my mind) ridiculously customized cars.

"Just ignore him," said Joey, accepting Wally's offer of a couple of crisps and awarding himself a handful that emptied the packet.

"You fucker," said Wally.

"Up yours," said Joey, who then proceeded to wipe his hands on Ronnie's denim jacket.

"Fuckin' 'ell," said Ronnie. "Me mum just washed that."

"Well, she'll have to wash it again, won't she?" said Joey. "Welcome to the ATC, mate. Anyway, John, it doesn't take brains to get ahead in this outfit. Dolly hasn't passed a fucking exam in his life, and look where he is. Pulls a lot of birds and all. Jammy bastard. I mean, fuck it, he's not even pretty."

"He doesn't have to be," said Wally, relieving Joey of his beret and throwing it across the room. "I know a girl in High Ongar whose sister says Dolly's got a plonker like a rhino's."

"So, John," said Joey, "the ATC's a bloody good lark. Fucking good summer camp last year, mate. At Linham . . ."

"Linham?" I wondered.

"Near Oxford," said Joey. "Transport Command."

"Yes," said Simon, with a rictus of disdain I understood. "Near Oxford. The place we're encouraged to 'aim for' at KEGS."

"That we are," I belched, momentarily looking, I can only suppose, depressed.

"Don't fucking give me that," said Simon. "You'll end up there. Guess what, you lot, not only is he good at Latin, he's taking Greek as well."

"Greek?" said Dolly, barging in with eyelids crimped and

mouth monumentally slack. "Going there on holiday or something?"

"Ancient Greek, you wanker," said Simon.

"I only bloody asked," said Dolly.

"Like I was saying, John," Joey continued, "Linham was good. Really fucking good. Up in the old Chipmunk. Bit of gliding. Loads of range time—.303s and SLRs."

"SLRs?" I was still a little preoccupied with Simon's assumption concerning my future.

"Self-loading rifle," said Dolly. "None of that .303 bolt-action bollocks. Stuff the clip in and get fucking going. Bang, bang, bang! Kicks like a bastard, mind you."

"Too bloody right," said Danny. He was barely literate (not that that troubled me), referred to kissing as "courting," and had spent his last year at Top School cleaning the windows, mowing the lawns, weeding the flowerbeds, and helping out in the kitchen. "I was in pain for a week."

"We had a crack at nine-mill, too, and all," continued Dolly.

"Nine . . . ?" I quizzed.

"Nine-mill," said Wally. "Pistol. Fucking useless. We all bloody missed by a mile."

"I fucking didn't," said Dolly.

"Oh, yes you did," said Wally. "What did the range sergeant say? 'This is a pistol. You will be disappointed. It takes a lot of practice. And we've only got half an hour.' "

"I did *not* fucking miss," said Dolly.

"Oh, yes you *did*," said Simon, said Wally, said Joey, in an ever-dependable, ever-reflexive reinvention of pantomime. "We were fucking there."

"Linham aside, John, and fuck off, Dolly," fumed Wally, "I wouldn't get your hopes up for this year's camp. We're bloody well stuck with some dopey fucking depot near Newcastle—big in 1940 but not anymore. 'Posting to nowhere,' Sticky calls it. Bloody cold, too, and not just in December. And Sticky ought to know. He was fucking well there in 1940."

Sticky wasn't kidding. RAF Ouston proved to be, as Joey gasped at the chilly commencement of a ten-minute march from barracks to breakfast on a cloudless Sunday in August, "England's fucking answer to the bloody North Pole."

He continued: "Why the fuck are we in shirtsleeve order?"

Wally responded: "Don't blame me. It was Sticky's idea."

This was, however, an inconvenience that I could now take in my stride. To Dad's amusement and Mum's despair, I'd fallen in love with the ATC and had now been in uniform (tailored down three sizes by Dad on our aging Singer) for three whole months. During that time, I had learned to coax a knife-edge crease into serge, to bring two boots to a state of radiance so pronounced that I could see every blemish on my face in their toecaps, to fire a Lee-Enfield .303 rifle without putting a bullet through a fellow cadet, to persuade a collar stud to do the job for which it had been designed, to about-turn on the march without tripping, to salute like a robot, and to recognize a hundred different aircraft from their silhouettes alone. (I had also become a fanatical aeromodeler and firm friends with Joey and Wally and Simon.)

I had, in fact, come to feel as effortlessly comfortable as I had upon meeting the rest of the Haney family for the first time nine years earlier. The regimentation, the sheer predictability, suited me down to the ground, standing as it did in blessed contradiction to the capriciousness of the KEGS regime (Ma Smith excepted) and the continuing uncertainties of life at home.

Ruined by civilian caterers the RAF had hired for the duration of Ouston's despoilment by a swarm of suppurating adolescents, breakfast, which we ate in the airmen's mess, was almost as mediocre as the one I'd disposed of on the way to Le Havre. There was, however, an imperishable supply of it—fatty bacon, cornflakes, Krispies, tinned tomatoes, porridge, scrambled eggs (genuine), twice-baked beans, fried bread, fifth-rate sausage. All of it was "shit," according to Dolly, compared to the food at Linham, and most of us were queasy by the time we got back to barracks for Sticky's "little chat" about the schedule for the week.

Later that day, after tea—rubbery beef, canned potatoes, and broad beans, followed by tinned rice pudding with a splatter of jam—we glibly received a completely unauthorized (and blatantly misleading) lecture on the fundamentals of gliding. It was delivered by an NCO from Debden, Sergeant Leslie Crowther, nicknamed Crackerjack—for, I surmised, the popular BBC children's television show of the same name hosted by another Leslie Crowther. Crackerjack, who bore a harrowing resemblance to the least attractive Bash Street Kid (a mutant named Plug) and had qualified to fly gliders solo, did his best to persuade those of us who had never been airborne that gliding was basically as safe as houses and that it only got "a bit fucking dodgy" if the cable connecting the glider to the winch broke before the glider had reached the altitude at which the cable was usually released.

(He was lying, as I later found out, purely to discountenance the new boys.)

"Which," he said, in between bites of a Mars Bar, "hardly ever happens. Once in a blue moon. Maybe."

"But what if it does?" chorused Sammy and Ronnie, neither of whom had been pleased to learn that one didn't wear a parachute when gliding.

"Well, it depends," said Crackerjack, who, after tea, had exchanged his uniform for an incredibly filthy flying suit.

"On what?"

"On exactly when it breaks." He grinned. "How fast you're going at the time. Because if you're not going fucking fast enough you might . . . er . . . how can I put this?"

"Stall," said Barry (Basher) Niven, a hard-nosed sergeant from Debden who was twice Dolly's size and headed the squadron's rifle-drill team. (That, too, was a lie.)

"Exactly," said Crackerjack. "You stall. And then you plummet. Possibly backwards. Which is not very nice. Not nice at all, in fact. But, like I said, cable breaks hardly ever happen."

ONE DID, HOWEVER, in my case—at twenty-five minutes past nine the following morning. (I have no idea why I looked at my watch.) Nursing numerous bruises and a nasty cut on the back of my neck (the latter induced by Wally in the course of the abject descent to jejune bestiality otherwise known as an ATC pillow fight), I was drinking in my very first aerial view of the land of my birth and also reflecting that the last time I'd seen anything remotely like it, I'd been full of *minestra di pasta grattata* and ecstatically positioned, all by myself, on a walkway at the breathtaking top of the Campanile in Siena. (This was on a ten-day school trip to Italy paid for by Mum.)

Suddenly, the two-seat open-cockpit glider in which Tim Talbot (the pilot) and I had previously been traveling so steadily onward and upward lurched to port, taking with it a smudge that might have been Newcastle.

"Cable break! Cable break! Oh . . . bugger!" said Tim, a middle-aged CI (and Anglican chorister) who lived in Saffron Walden. "Get your head between your knees, lad—now, for Christ's sake! Not next fucking week!"

Forcing my head forward as far as it would go, I stared in stupefaction at the floor while Tim briskly tinkered with joystick and rudder bar in search of a rate of descent worthy of description as more or less controlled. A few long seconds later, he announced that we might be in for a bit of a bumpy landing, at which point I allowed myself a cockeyed glance over the side as terra (all too) firma came rushing up to meet us.

The glider hit the topsoil with a thud that gave me a universal toothache for a couple of minutes. Once it had skittered and skinked to a stop, I extracted myself from the cockpit with as much esprit as I could muster and awaited the arrival of the cadets who had been detailed to lug the contraption back to dispersal. The first to turn up was a leering Basher, followed by a giggling Wally, a smirking Joey, and a sniggering Crackerjack (who'd been roundly berated by Tim for some slipshod flying earlier in the day).

"You," said Basher, "are as white as a fucking sheet."

"How surprising is that?" I yapped. " 'Once in a blue moon'? Bollocks."

At this point, Tim came by at a pious (and, I thought, hypocritical) clip to stamp on all the swearing.

Subsiding into silence, I suddenly realized that Joey was gazing, for no apparent reason, at my crotch.

"What's your fucking problem?" I barked.

"Oh, nothing much," said Joey. "We had a bet on."

"A bet? What kind of bet?"

"On whether or not you'd wet yourself when things got a little bit iffy," said Basher. "So, unless you're wearing nappies, I've just won five bob."

Half an hour later, we went up again. The indiscriminate smudge reappeared, the sun came out, and I was adrift, now and forever it somehow seemed, a thousand feet above the country that Grandpa and Dad had fought for.

"Good fun, eh?" said Tim, as a thermal nudged us closer to the clouds.

"Yes," I simpered in sheer elation. "Bloody good fun—really good."

"Yes," echoed Tim, with the ghost of a smile. "Bloody good fun. Bloody good fun indeed."

A few minutes later, he turned for home.

"Mustn't miss this afternoon's 'interest visit.' "

"Will it be interesting?" I asked.

"Only," said Tim, "if something goes horribly wrong."

THE PLACE OF INTEREST turned out to be the test range at Spadeadam, where we stood in a bunker with extremely thick walls and watched a static firing of a rocket engine originally intended for the Blue Streak, the British ICBM that, because of cost overruns, never quite happened. Once what little smoke there was had cleared, Basher muttered: "Really fucking boring."

The rest of the week proved considerably more dramatic. The Soviets invaded Czechoslovakia, the RAF went to twenty-four-hour standby, and Crackerjack almost broke a glider with yet another of the high-speed landings for which he was now notorious. Wally and Simon bagged a twenty-minute ride in a helicopter, Joey went up for two hours in a visiting Vickers Varsity (a navigational trainer), I almost drowned while not quite failing to gain a certificate of proficiency in swimming, the quality of the food in the airmen's mess went from bad to worse, and Dolly was threatened with demotion on the train back to London for "courting" in uniform.

CHAPTER 8

Greasy Grub and Gliding

. . . .

BY THE BEGINNING OF 1971—I WAS NOW SEVENTEEN—BASHER was a cadet warrant officer and Joey and Simon were sergeants. I, for my part, had been promoted to corporal and grown adept at shrieking orders clearly in a crosswind. (Sticky and Tiny were quite impressed.) Crackerjack had just applied to join the Royal Marines.

We had also attended three more summer camps. The first: in Cornwall, at RAF St. Mawgan (a frontline maritime patrol operation fielding a prop-driven relic called the Shackleton and its up-to-date successor, the jet-propelled and problematic Nimrod). The second: at RAF Binbrook, a Strike Command base fielding both the English Electric Lightning (an insanely overpowered interceptor) and the Canberra (a photorecon-naissance aircraft, slightly long in the tooth by then). The third: at RAF Coningsby (deep in the flat-as-a-pancake Mid-lands), where the food was "more than halfway fucking decent for a change" (as Joey put it) and people were learning to fly and direct, sometimes at speeds in excess of Mach 2, the truly formidable Phantom (nuclear bombs and less fearsome explosives expelled at the drop of a headset). Also at Coningsby, I had almost howled for joy while sitting in a Chipmunk as it rattled and skidded and side-slipped and soared, through no fault of its own, ten thousand feet up, in the wake of a passing Vulcan nuclear bomber, a triangular bat out of fissile hell with the power to liquefy every last window in Leningrad. ("In case you were wondering, they did that on purpose," said the Chipmunk's saturnine pilot, an RAF squadron leader who had once flown Lightnings. "It's their idea of a joke.")

I had rarely been happier.

AT THE SAME TIME, however, I knew that my days in the ATC must come to a close. I had, in 1970, gained enough O Levels to secure admission to the sixth form and, therefore, to specialization in the only subjects I liked: English, Greek, and Latin. Wading through Austen, *The Waste Land,* Jonson, bits of the *Iliad* (Books XXII and XXIV, to be exact), Tacitus, and *King Lear* now entailed a minimum of twenty-five hours of homework every week. It would, I thought with considerable regret, soon be time to resign.

Everything went awry, however, one Friday in March, when Sticky turned up during tea break and announced that the West Essex Wing of the ATC would be staging an assault-course competition during the upcoming North Weald Air Show and, furthermore, that the winning team would get to have tea in a mess hall for visiting aircrew. Sticky asked for volunteers and my hand went up in a trice.

"That's very nice of you, Corporal Haney," said Sticky,

polishing off a burger. "But you needn't have bothered. You're in charge anyway."

"Really, sir?" I said.

"Yes," said Sticky. "Really. And Corporal Battiscombe will be your deputy." At which point, I reminded myself that Lionel Battiscombe, though a good egg in general, wasn't remotely combative. Even worse, he'd played the prig upon learning (this was at RAF Coningsby) that Phantom pilots taxiing past the air traffic control tower always extended the aircraft's refueling probe whenever they knew that an unusually desirable Women's Royal Air Force officer happened to be on duty inside.

EVERY SUNDAY MORNING for the next two months, the members of the assault-course team, dressed in baggy overalls and therefore resembling nothing so much as the proverbial sacks of shit tied up in the middle with string, hurled themselves at (but not always over) nine-foot walls, clambered up thirty feet of netting and back down the other side, tiptoed briskly along foot-wide planks set ten feet off the ground, and wriggled as fast as they could along a shallow slit trench roofed with a hedge of barbed wire. As the weeks passed, Corporal Haney and Corporal Battiscombe, to their own amazement and Sticky's, started to get results. The team's course-completion time fell steadily, and by the final weekend before the air show, it had begun to look as though we might not quite disgrace ourselves.

The rest of the squadron wasn't so sure.

THE DAY OF DECISION started badly. Sticky and Bighead repaired to the refreshment tent well before lunch, drank too much beer, and shortly thereafter fell off a total of four BSA motorbikes in the space of exactly five minutes. Two hours later, Basher dropped his rifle just seconds from the end of what would otherwise have been a flawless drill display.

"Fuck me," said Joey, rubbing his eyes in disbelief. "Did what I think just happened really happen?"

"I'm afraid it fucking did," said Wally.

"Made the fucking crowd laugh," I muttered, lighting up a Player's No. 6. "Bloody bad luck, that. Basher's been working his balls off for weeks."

"And fuck-all good will it do him," said Danny. "Sticky and Bighead'll go completely fucking mental. He's in for a right old bollocking."

"Huh!" said Joey. "Me too and all, if the bike display gets messed up."

"It won't," said Wally.

"It fucking might," said Joey.

"Cheer up, lads," I said sourly. "Even if the bike team does fall flat on its horrible fucking face, there's always a chance—a fucking remote one, I know—that me and Lionel might win the assault-course contest."

"Fat chance," said Crackerjack.

AT HALF PAST TWO, Lionel and I and the other eight cadets in the team donned our overalls and marched over to the agglomeration of wood, rope, and wire we had come to know so well. I then reported to the chief steward, a CI from a squadron with which we had almost come to blows during a soccer tournament at Coningsby. "Oh, yes, 424," he said. "I remember you lot, bunch of fucking fairies from Debden. Guess what—you're up last."

When I got back to my teammates, I discovered that in my absence Lionel had begun to undermine morale by claiming that our opponents looked unbeatable. Conceding the point that every cadet in the other nine teams looked just like the worst kind of yob, I immediately reminded him that none of them had trained on the North Weald course.

"So what?" he said.

"So what?" I snapped. "I'll tell you so fucking what. We know this course inside out and the other fuckers don't."

"So?"

"So we might have an unfair advantage," I said. "Possibly."

"Oh," said Lionel. "Brains over brawn?"

"Brains?" I replied. "You must be joking. When was the last time you saw someone using their bloody brains in the ATC?"

THROUGHOUT THE HOUR AND A HALF it took the other teams to compete, Lionel oscillated between getting upset whenever the enemy fired off a barrage of insults and complaining about the fact that the contest, far from being the sideshow he'd expected, had begun to attract a surprisingly large and curious crowd. The rest of the team ignored him (on my orders) and surreptitiously chain-smoked while staring at the aerial entertainment.

The RAF display team, the Red Arrows, naturally provoked the hysterical typhoon of postimperial oohs and patriotic aahs that greets their every appearance, zooming through the heavens in perfect formation at five hundred miles an hour. Shrieks of amazement erupted when a Lightning went up in a vertical climb so incredibly fast that it vanished from sight in mere seconds. And perhaps the most engaging and strangely graceful demonstration of the day was given by the Royal Belgian Air Force team, who were flying the Fouga Magister, an odd-looking plane (nicknamed the Whistling Turtle) that sang where others screamed.

SHORTLY AFTER THE BELGIANS HAD LANDED, reality reintroduced itself. Having arrived at the start line, I was taken aside by a steward and brusquely informed that I couldn't compete in sneakers.

"It's boots or black shoes only, sonny."

This was news to me, and the situation wasn't exactly improved when the chief steward picked up his megaphone and demanded to know what the hell 424 ("a bunch of old women") thought they were doing and were we going to go around the course or not? My boots were back in the squadron coach, which was parked half a mile away. The problem was solved, incompletely, when another steward removed his winklepickers, which were recognizably black and repulsively dirty, and told me to put them on.

"What size are they?" I inquired.

"Ten. What size do you take?"

"Eight."

"Hard fucking cheese, mate."

I duly trudged back to the start line, my footwear making a flopping noise, and pulled the team into a muddle for a last-minute near total rethink of strategy.

"Sammy has to lead this time," I said.

"Why Sammy?" said Lionel, looking thoroughly offended. "I'm second in fucking command here."

"Because," I said, "he's second fucking fastest after me, you prat, that's why, and I'm completely buggered in these boots."

THE STARTING PISTOL popped and we darted forward like partridges beaten from cover. All I remember about the next few minutes is the astonishing pain in my feet and legs and the sound of a two-foot gash being torn in my overalls as I sprinted on my stomach at the bottom of the trench. Sammy came in first and I came in second with the rest of the team right behind me.

"That was fast, Corporal," said Bighead. "Extremely fast. I was timing you."

While the timekeepers tallied the results, we watched as a Vulcan made a low pass, stood on its tail, and went to full power (eighty-eight thousand screeching pounds of catastrophic thrust), a rehearsal for horror I'd seen twice before. My ears were therefore still ringing twenty minutes later when, along with everyone else, the CI who had, so very recently, seen fit to dismiss my confreres and me as a sodality of shirt-lifters, heard the announcement that 424 had won.

Too surprised to look pleased, my teammates and I, having changed back into razor-sharp creases, were each awarded a chintzy shield, inscribed with the insignia of the ATC, by an air vice marshal (extremely retired) who looked old enough to have test-flown the S.E.5a. We then strode off to the promised land, to the prize for which we had fought so hard that the aches and pains lasted a fortnight.

Which turned out to be a grubby canteen staffed by civil-ian caterers. Not much of an advertisement, I thought to my-self, for the British commitment to NATO. Making the best of a bad job, we tucked into beefburgers, chips, and baked beans while looking in vain for the pilots whose company we had been promised. Just as we were about to leave, the Belgians walked in, oozing élan from every pore of their flying suits— the right stuff minus a space program.

Soon, though, being Continentals, they became conspicu-ously dissatisfied with the food. The least I could do, I thought, was to let them know exactly how much I'd enjoyed their performance. The few words I spoke as a consequence earned me, however, the frightening sight of a perfectly syn-chronized partial rotation of severely cropped heads and a measured response from a thickset man with the face of a psy-chopathic otter, eyes the color of antifreeze, and epaulettes in-dicative of absolute command.

"Sank you, Corporal, sank you very much," he said. "But I am curious. How would you describe sis . . . sis stuff we have to eat?"

"I'm terribly sorry about that, sir," I said. "I'm afraid it's what we're used to. Welcome to England."

UPON ARRIVING HOME, I showed my shield to an unimpressed Mum (who was knitting an arty jumper for Joy and listening to Pentangle), made myself a bacon sandwich, took a bath, disinfected those cuts that still looked unhappy, limped into my bedroom, skimmed half a page of *Paradise Lost*, sketched a translation of six lines of Pindar, worked for an hour on an essay in progress on *Persuasion*, made myself another bacon sandwich, and, at about ten, fell into bed with a copy of *Put Out More Flags.*

Shortly before midnight, Dad, back from a late shift, looked in to ask me how things had gone.

"We won," I said.

"You're joking. Really? Well done."

"Thanks. But I'm leaving. No more ATC for me. It's getting in the way of all this homework. I'll give it a few more months. Until the end of the school year. And that'll be that."

"Will you miss it?"

"Yes," I said. "I will."

"It's funny," said Dad. "I never quite thought it would suit you."

"Well, it did," I replied.

"So what was it?" said Dad. "Greasy grub and gliding?"

"No," I responded.

Dad raised an eyebrow.

"Look at it this way. There's sixty of us. More or less. And not a snob in sight."

"Hmmm," said Dad. "So . . . that means a lot to you?"

"Of course it does," I replied. "It's a damned sight better than the high-and-mighty attitudes at school. The ATC—well, 424—is all right, mate. Bit rough-and-ready—and guess what? I like that. And pretty bloody working-class. Taken as a whole. Including the officers. None of whom were officers during the war. Sticky and Bighead were only ground crew. And Tiny drove staff cars somewhere. Palestine, I think."

"I wouldn't call Joey working-class," said Dad. "Look at the palace he lives in."

"I know that, Dad," I sighed. "But I said 'as a *whole.*' There's only one Joey in the whole bloody bunch. And he's about as bloody un-snobbish as they come. Joy's actually rather keen on him."

"Really?" said Dad.

"Yes," I said. "She is—and we all know how much time she has for toffee-nosed gits. And there's no racial prejudice, either. (Well, almost none. Dolly gets a bit worked up—fuck knows why—at times.) So there's three black blokes in our crowd. And they're popular. Are there any blacks at KEGS? Not that I've noticed. And the only Jew and the only Muslim—Pakistani bloke—at school . . . well, let's just say they haven't been made what I'd call terribly welcome."

"Hmmm," said Dad. "That doesn't surprise me. Always thought that place was a bit old-fashioned."

"Oh, it's worse than that," I said. "It's hopelessly provincial. Like everything else about Chelmsford."

A FRIDAY EVENING three months later witnessed the solemn return of my ATC garb (battledress, greatcoat, malformed beret, two collarless light-blue shirts) to the quartermaster's store, an asylum of rifles and somnolent spiders overseen in theory and neglected in practice by Simon.

"Well, well, well," he said, closing the door on a dozen D.P. ("demonstration purposes") Lee-Enfield .303s. "I suppose that's that."

"I suppose it is," I said, waving limply at Danny, at Dolly (who, having worked his way back into favor with the squadron commander, now wore an adult warrant officer's uniform), and at Little Jimmy Rutherford, Tiny's son, who had embarrassed us all on the twenty-five-yard range at St. Mawgan by dropping a loaded pistol.

"What are you doing in that poxy get-up?" said Dolly, passing summary judgment on my navy suede shoes, maroon crushed-velvet loon pants, and dirty-blond Third World First T-shirt. "You look a right cunt in that lot."

"He's leaving," said Simon.

"Leaving?" snarled Dolly, piggy eyes pared down to perfect hyphens. "Leaving? You fucking deserter."

"I'm terribly sorry, Dolly," I replied in the asinine mix of Nicholas Featherstone *furens* and Mott the Hoople fanatic that passed for purebred English in the cheap seats at the Bell, the Two Brewers, the Stag, the Red Cow, the Woodman, the Cock, and the several other drinking troughs in and around Ongar where I had by now begun to acquire a passion for hybridized whiskey, Guinness on tap, and short-winded small talk with muddy-cuffed maestros of hedging and ditching who ate with their mouths open, rarely bathed, and were expert at mating in haystacks. "Exams to pass. That sort of thing."

"Going to university, are we?" said Dolly, hitting his contrary stride.

"Maybe."

"Well, if you do, mate, don't forget who's fucking well paying for it. Poor sods like me." (Which, inasmuch as Dolly had recently landed a job that required him to wear a suit, was true.) "The British bloody taxpayer."

"Put a fucking sock in it, you two," said Simon. "And by the way, John, Tiny wants to see you."

"Really?" I asked. "Why?"

"I don't fucking know," he said. "Probably can't wait to thank you for all the good work. The brilliant bit of map-reading by you and Lionel that got us all lost in the middle of nowhere last year."

"You didn't have to bring that up."

"Just couldn't fucking resist it."

"I told Sticky I couldn't read a map to save my life. It's not my fucking fault he didn't believe me."

"And what," said Dolly, who hadn't finished, "is Third World fucking First when it's at home?"

"Er . . . it's an organization that raises people's awareness about the poorer parts of the world," I replied, suddenly wishing I'd never been talked into joining by my friend Anthony Parker, a neighborhood Maoist and Brentwood success who had recently introduced me to the flashback cavatinas of the Doors and also to the work of Herbert Marcuse, whom I found incomprehensible but persisted with because my descents upon Anthony's lounge for a double dose of *Strange Days* and armchair analysis of industrial unrest in Bolivia usually afforded me a mesmeric aperçu of his wasp-waisted sibling, a not-quite-flat-chested leftist Antigone named Viv.

"Africa? That sort of thing?" snorted Dolly. "The nig-nogs?"

"Yes, Dolly, the nig-nogs," I groaned, "and every other flat-broke wog you'd care to bloody mention."

"I see," said Dolly. "So is it working?"

"Is what working?"

"Third World First."

"I don't fucking know."

"So why are you in it?"

"I'll tell you why," said Simon, who knew nothing about politics. "He fancies the tart who flogged him the shirt something fucking chronic. Funny thing is, Viv's got no knockers and he's a bit of a tit man."

"A bit?" said Dolly, basing his disbelief on my attraction

to Vicki (who, to the nasal accompaniment of *Tea for the Tillerman*, had finally removed all her clothing for me a couple of weekends earlier). "A bit? He's a fucking pervert."

"I can be flexible," I said, remembering exactly how Viv had looked at Vicki's sixteenth birthday party, bouncing around to a Jeff Beck anthem in something that turned out to be semi-see-through whenever she was backlit. "Very flexible."

ALTHOUGH GRAMMAR-SCHOOL TYPES tended to make him uncomfortable, Tiny blithered on about nothing for more than half an hour and even suggested that I stay for one last beefburger, a proposition I declined in favor of extending a farewell to Edna, who was deftly displacing yards and yards of plastic wrap from several fork-resistant clots of still part-frozen beef patties. Then I returned to No. 13 to wrestle with the final fifty lines of Book VI of the *Aeneid*.

This, however, was a project I shelved when I found a note taped to the tea caddy.

GONE TO JENNIE'S

JOY AT SKIPTONS' WITH SANDY

DAD AT THE OFFICE

Which meant that Mum was hanging out with her best friend and putting up with commercial TV without bitching (as she usually did at home) about the inanity of the ads, that Joy and her best friend, Sandra Finch, were imitating star-crossed lovers under Phil's direction, and that Dad (who had recently taught himself the essentials of caring for mainframe computers) had been awarded yet another stint of overtime.

Virgil could wait. I swallowed some tinned spaghetti and dashed into the living room to indulge a relatively newfound obsession: playing "drums" with the assistance of the arm of an easy chair and a pair of knitting needles.

By the time Mum came home, at ten, to a pile of washing-up I'd promised to attend to but hadn't, our secondhand stereo was going full blast, I was looking as disheveled from the collarbone up as one ever can when sporting a military haircut, and the floor was littered with a selection of LPs evidencing my inconsistent musical proclivities: Fairport Convention's *Unhalfbricking*, the Beach Boys' *Surf's Up*, Bowie's *Changes*, *Led Zeppelin II*, the Keith Tippett Group's *Dedicated to You, But You Weren't Listening*, and Duke Ellington's *New Orleans Suite* (the latter on loan from Jeremy Jones, a fellow KEGS classicist).

I was also, unfortunately, halfway through side one of an album by a "progressive jazz" ensemble Mum loathed but longed to like because the *Guardian* gave them good reviews.

"Oh, God, not Soft Machine again," she said.

"Sorry, Mum. Jeremy seems to think they're terribly brainy. And Jeremy being a bit of a brain, he's almost certainly right."

"Oh," she said. "I see."

I lit a measly cigarette, sucked very hard, and started to cough like a cat crossing swords with an exceptionally unforgiving hairball.

"I'd quite like a cigarette," said Mum.

"Are you sure about that?" I wheezed, extending the packet.

"Oh," she said with a scandalized shudder. "Number 10. Ugh." (The No. 10 was the No. 6's conspicuously poorer cousin. Few cigarettes were cheaper.)

"How about a French cig instead?" I rejoined, plumbing the depths of the tangle of torn leather, Scotch tape, and shoe-mending glue otherwise known as my briefcase for what proved to be the only undamaged Gitane in a battered blue packet. "I know you like those, dear. Very Mrs. Jean-Paul Sartre." (Mum was, at this stage, inexplicably obsessed with De Beauvoir.)

Joy, peasant dress streaming from snowdrop-white shoulders, burst in and sighed: " 'Then, window, let day in, and let life out.' " A quickstep behind her, in a caftan, came Sandy, who croaked, " 'Farewell, farewell,' " then burped and apologized—"Ever so sorry, Mrs. Haney, must've 'ad too much cake at Mrs. Skipton's"—and hiccupped, " 'One kiss, and I'll'—" She looked befuddled.

". . . and . . . ?" said Joy.

" 'I'll descend,' " said Mum. "And don't look so surprised, John. I haven't forgotten everything I learned at school, you know—and, by the way, do the words 'washing' and 'up' ring a bell?"

"Can't it wait?" I muttered. "There's something I want to listen to on the radio in a minute."

"Like what?" said Mum.

"Music," I growled.

"What kind of music?"

"Leonard Bernstein."

"Anything I'm familiar with?" said Mum, who was keen on *West Side Story.*

"No," I replied. "It's a symphony of sorts based on a Jewish funeral prayer."

"Ooh, that sounds lovely," Juliet murmured, barely concealing a smirk. "A fun-filled end to a glorious day. I just can't wait—what do you think, Sandy?"

Sandy, a congenital comic with spinach-green teeth, a sandpiper's ankles, and the skin tones of an oyster—promptly took Juliet's side.

Outvoted thus, I did "the Fairy Liquid dance" (as Joy had dubbed it when tiny) and duly dropped a varicose plate, a mishandled mug, and a saucer. At midnight, the thrum and consumptive surcease of a Prefect in need of a tune-up, followed by the clink of a half-asleep key in the lock of our testy front door, announced the return of Dad to his castle, his chancel, his place of intermittent repose and unperfected rest.

CHAPTER 9

The Birthplace of Toad-in-the-Hole

. . . .

FOUR YEARS LATER, ON A COLD DECEMBER EVENING, I SEE-
sawed through the back door at No. 13 in stack-heeled boots,
sixth form scarf, Blind Faith tee, combat jacket, and Army
surplus greatcoat, groggily mouthing the words to a Sensa-
tional Alex Harvey Band song titled "Gang Bang." I was, at
this time, close to completing, with minimal aplomb and a lot
of last-minute revision, a B.A. in classics at the University of
London's least refined and most remote outpost. Royal Holloway College overlooked Egham, a small town in Surrey; it
was generally known as RHC (and also as "Royal Holiday
College") to the THBs—meaning "typical Holloway blokes"
and "typical Holloway birds"—who, at least in theory, studied there.

I now remember RHC—or, rather, its centerpiece, the
Founder's Building—as a Victorian pile that stank (on a bad
day) of overcooked cabbage, congealed baked beans, chocolate biscuits, burning toast, patchouli oil, and nonstop forni-

cation. It also looked a bit like Chenonceau or a ziggurat of gingerbread spattered with marzipan icing, depending on how much beer I'd had for supper and how much sex I'd had the night before with my very first serious girlfriend, a good-natured registered nurse named Helen Pryor. Her father, a Black Label–swilling Brazilian of Cornish extraction, worked for the BBC World Service, smoked Du Maurier cigarettes (a bourgeois brand), dwelt amid doctors (and dentists and spies), and, like his prim, when minus gin, but kindly English wife, always made me welcome in his well-appointed home in Hertfordshire. This although he was, I think, a bit disturbed by the length of my hair (about two feet), the cut of my jeans, and the indeterminate nature of my background.

I had, a few hours earlier, enjoyed an unbalanced lunch consisting of two cans of Foster's, a packet of peanuts, a

Vacationing in Devon, 1974

double Black Russian, a half-pint glass of Bull's Blood (a rotgut Hungarian *rouge*), an enervated bacon roll, an even more lethargic individual apple pie, and a brief but euphoric encounter (behind Helen's back) with a previously distant acquaintance named Cecile—a Belgian woman with a face like a horse and a figure like Twiggy's who was taken with the fact that I had read, or so I said, *D'Alembert's Dream* and not quite all of *Jacques le fataliste*. Partly undone by this minor debauch, I dumped my gargantuan rucksack (crammed with laundry, *Howards End*, a bass drum pedal, *The Club of Queer Trades*, and a box of Ritmeester cigars from Jackie's lover) somewhere in the hall and clomped into the living room. There I learned, from a dumbstruck Mum and a blubbering Joy, that Sandy had died two days ago of kidney failure diagnosed as something unimportant.

" '. . .wherefore art thou Romeo?' " I thought to myself, sitting down with a drunken thud.

"You look terrible," said Mum.

"I always dress like this," I said. "Have they shot her doctor yet?"

"No," said Mum, "but they should. And cut out the jokes. You really do look dreadful. I honestly think you ought to go to bed."

Which I did. There, while waiting for the walls to settle down, I wondered what it was that D'Alembert had dreamed of, ruminated on why Cecile appeared to like me, reminded myself that Helen probably liked me even more, meditated on whether to tell my parents that I was now toying with the idea of absconding to the capital after graduation with a view to securing a toehold in music (I had now been playing drums for two years in pickup bands at college), and puzzled on how Joy would fare in the absence of her closest female friend.

THE ANSWER TO THE LAST (and by far the most momentous) question came six months later. Joy had been finishing a foundation program in fine arts; she now abandoned both it and her very first serious boyfriend, Andrew Palmer. Andy was a gifted painter, offbeat wit, gregarious son of a West Country lawyer, and the only product of a fee-paying school I'd ever met who wasn't at all snobbish. Joy dropped him in order to announce her intention to marry a heavily bearded, hugely bespectacled barkeep from Arizona (by my speculation, a listless practitioner of New Age indisciplines, everything Andy, whom Mum and Dad idolized, wasn't) named Barney. Joy and Andy had met him during a camping holiday in the Peloponnese, where she had acquired a love of kasseri and a sensible aversion to the battery acid the Greeks so very shamelessly passed off as wine back then.

My parents' own marriage (though no longer marred by the overt antipathy that had once inspired my fully damped fantasias of defecting to the inlet of orzo and Boursin next door) was, by now, within a year of failing altogether. They chose, to my amazement, not to oppose the mésalliance. Instead, they sent out a neutral communiqué noting the imminence of a ceremony whose only merit, in my eyes, was the opportunity it would give "all of us" to congregate for the first time since cousin Pauline's nuptials, in 1966, when Dad had looked pensive (and Mum had looked away) when Joan could no longer stand up.

WHAT WAS (and remains) a day whose deficiencies I doubt that I'll ever forget began with a discharge of high-summer bird-song that, due to a hangover, I found every bit as earsplitting as the intestinal scream excreted by a Phantom. Once trapped in Levi's and a Thin Lizzy T-shirt and, to the tune of the mystified tick and the mortified tock of my thunderstruck discount alarm, increasingly disturbed by the fact that my fate's next accompli would come in the form of an unwanted brother-in-law, I plodded step by step down the echoing stairs, whose carpet, rattled and banged in recent days by Mum with the aid of an elderly hoover, was still the pitiful color of cut-price mustard.

Dad was, of course, in the kitchen, sequestered with a bubbling cup of Brooke Bond and a Rothmans Select. (No wedding worth its salt could take place without a spiky spray of high-end cigarettes in a polished glass on every table.) Joy, pale and thin and dressed in jeans and a Wishbone Ash T-shirt, looked strangely detached, as if she wanted nothing more than to fly away forever. (Dad confided to me later that he had told her, the previous evening, that she didn't have to go through with it.) Mum, in the lounge, was striking unswervingly hard with a well-directed iron at the plain white hippie dress that Joy had selected for the bleating of her matrimonial vows.

Two mugs of coffee, ten No. 6, and a handful of painkillers later, I set about flattening my "interview suit." This three-piece affront to high style came from the Moorgate branch of

Hornes, a semiprecious series of "better" men's clothiers where Dad, Dick, and Dave often shopped. While thus enraged, I also rehearsed, with bridled tongue and G-clamped teeth, the fictive tirade in defense of disaster with which, as best man, I'd soon be obliged to despoil the garden-party portion of the coming afternoon.

At about eleven-thirty, Helen, who had come down from London by train—she was working at University College Hospital—flounced up the front-garden path in a form-fitting dress (pitch-black with motif of red feathers) I thought more suited to breaking the ice at an orgy, an Ossie Clark number not only permitting the global exposure of a staggering proportion of her not inconsiderable cleavage but also enabling, from the rear, the effortless display of an equally arresting length of leg by dint of an unsubtle slit up the back that stopped an inch short of an open invitation to delirium. Not too far behind her, in Sunday best (Tootal, Viyella, and crimplene) and looking nervous, came Rose and Don and their children.

Having introduced Helen to the Harbinger Road contingent, I gently marched her into the back garden, where, a few feet from the compost heap and the rockery, I ignited a Benson & Hedges and hissed: "Did you have to wear that fucking dress today?"

"I thought it might cheer you up," she grinned, making an unnecessary adjustment to her attire that entailed an inflation of uplift.

"Oh, it's cheered me up all right," I gasped, remembering the first time I'd seen her in it, at a party at the home for the disabled where, hoping to make myself useful for once, I'd worked as a care assistant in between leaving KEGS and going to university.

"So," she continued, "that was the Isle of Dogs lot, right? The life and soul of the tribe you say you belong to, the pie-and-mash crowd, the people you never mentioned at school. Correct? Or to me. At first."

"Yes," I said, "that was the Isle of Dogs lot, otherwise known as Mr. and Mrs. Donald Haney and their two lovely daughters, Susan and Diane. What tipped you off, honey bunny? It's not as if they're brandishing placards announcing the fact."

"It was the way you slipped into Cockney when you said hello to Don. That, plus I already knew that Rose and Don have two small kids and Dave and Ena have one, who's older than you."

"Leave it out, you silly cow," I said without a second thought despite the fact that what she'd said about my brief dalliance with the dialect of the East End was true. "I've only got one accent. Ongar with unseen translation thrown in. Grammar school with, here and there, a cowpat."

"Now, look," said Helen. "I'm not bloody making that up. It's also the way you talk sometimes when you're blotto, when you're so fucking sloshed, so full of scotch and Colt 45 that, when I do this, not too bloody much happens."

So saying, she mirrored her prior performance but this time combined it with the centrifugal shimmy that had always left me lopped off at the knees when we were alone and I was sober.

"It's a bloody good job you've got your back to the house," I croaked. "And I know you're not making it up, but does it really matter? And who the fuck cares?"

"I do," she said.

"I know you do," I replied, remembering how valiantly

she'd often dealt with my craving for whelks whenever they were poisoned.

DICK, NOT YET SCARLET, and Joan, at an angle, filtered onto the patio. They were followed by Dave (in a most subdued suit) and Ena (now slowing but never more stately), cousin Pauline (and her side-splitting husband, a master plumber we all called "young Dave" to set him apart from his father-in-law), Dave and Pauline's daughters (Wendy and Gillian) in matching boxy frocks, Ray (cracking a joke) and Eileen, and Dad (in a silver-gray two-piece I coveted) and Mum, weakly smiling and worried.

"So," said Helen, "aren't you going to introduce me to the rest of them?"

"Only if you promise not to keep hitching your tits up every ten seconds."

It came as no surprise to me that Dick (who had once been reproached by a blow from Joan's purse for dancing too voraciously with Mum at a "bit of a shindig" in Stratford) took a liking to Helen. Shortly before he died, six years later, he asked whether she and I were still together.

BY THE TIME WE RETURNED from St. Mary's, in High Ongar, my grammar-school accent was close to collapse. Don, in the dining room and momentarily solo, was looking, rather dubiously (a can of Double Diamond in one hand, an Embassy phosphorescing in the other), at the catered buffet, which consisted of the kind of topless cheese tart (with a very French name) that I had first been subjected to by Helen.

"Oh God, not bloody quiche," I snarled.

"So that's what it looks like," said Don. "Is it any good?"

"No it bloody isn't," I responded. "It's runny fucking cheese in a pie shell. . . . I mean, what's the point? This is all Elizabeth David's fault. Want to know what I could use? A really big ham sandwich." (I had recently skimmed Mum's newly purchased copy of Elizabeth David's *A Book of Mediterranean Food*.)

"A lovely ham sandwich," hummed Don. "Wouldn't say no. Do you fancy a beer?"

"Of course I do," I said, "and I'm bloody well going to need it."

"Really?"

"I've got to make the best man's speech. Dearly beloved, isn't this wonderful, good luck to both of you, we're all so happy, we're really not losing a daughter but gaining a son . . ."

"That's what's your dad's supposed to say," said Don.

"Oh, dear, you're right."

PARTLY PROPPED UP by the north-facing wall of our pine-and-asbestos garage, I spoke insincerely to relatives and neighbors of sweetness and light to a trickle of courteous applause. Once done with false witness and having, as I'd expected, had my oration succinctly maligned by a friend of Joy's, an arty (and arrogant) writer of sorts who had sold his soul to the gospel of macrobiotics, as "a load of balls," I opened a bottle of Stella Artois, borrowed a Rothmans from Dad, and sidled over to Helen.

She was talking to Ray and had, I found out, been apprised

of many things: the state of the public baths in Plaistow in the '30s (towels like sandpaper; lather-free soap; dismissive attendants), and of seeing a bus he and Dad had just missed reduced in a flash to four wheels and corpses.

"They're all very nice," she said several hours later, as the infelicities were drawing to a close. "But, well, oh, I don't know, maybe a little bit clannish. They mix well—and yet . . ."

"They stand out a bit in a non-Cockney crowd?" I said. "Of course they do. I suppose you could call that clannish, in a way. Suits me, though. You know, I sometimes think I'd be bloody well lost without them. Even though we hardly ever see them."

"Were they really that poor?" she asked.

"Of course they bloody were," I replied with a certain class-conscious defensiveness that Helen often found tiresome.

"Don't be so touchy," said Helen.

"I am *not* being touchy," I muttered, biting my tongue and reminding myself that it wasn't really Helen's fault that from her point of view the Cockneys (and various bits and pieces of me) came from another planet.

"Dick seemed quite jolly," she offered.

"He can be extremely jolly, genuinely witty, and ever so engaging. As he was when he was talking to you. He is, after all, love, a pretty successful salesman. But that was about four hours ago and he's as pissed as a fucking newt right now. And so, I'm afraid, is Joan."

"She seems kind," said Helen. "And a bit of a laugh."

"They're all very kind," I said sternly. "They're the kindest people I know. And Joan can, indeed, be a giggle. But not with a dozen gins inside her."

"It's odd," said Helen, "that Dick and Joan are the only ones overdoing it."

"Well," I said, "Joy has a theory—well, no, I think it's Dad's. I never asked him. But she did."

"And?"

"In Dick's case, sweet Fanny Adams for Christmas, losing their father when they were just nippers, life at the orphanage, walking to work at the poor old Commercial as youngsters because they didn't have the bus fare, and, I'm afraid, sometimes going pretty fucking hungry. I could go on forever, but I won't. Didn't worry Dad, didn't worry Dave, didn't worry Ray, didn't worry Don. Well, not too much."

"But Dick?"

"Dad thinks it broke him. He's a serious alcoholic, Helen. Fucking serious. And Joanie's in there with him."

"Oh," said Helen. "Oh—I see."

DICK, NOW RED-FACED AND SWEATING, and Joan, not quite on all fours, were almost the last to leave, and, when they did, were squabbling so loudly and venomously that No. 13's three remaining inhabitants smelled the rat of condescension for several weeks thereafter whenever our paths and those of our neighbors ran parallel. An hour or so later, my parents, unspeakably glum and fatigued, retreated (Dad with a lump of Cheddar, Mum with a pound of the peerless fudge in which she took refuge when frightened) to their separate beds.

At midnight, Helen and I went through the motions of propriety, as we always did whenever she came to stay. She slept in my bed, while I withdrew to a sleeping bag in the lounge. Two hours later, she tiptoed barefoot down the stairs, took off her nightie, and woke me up for some suitably shameless indulgence in the ticklish divertissement referred to, in the birthplace of toad-in-the-hole, as a "quick one."

"Fuck me, you're on form tonight," I whispered as we unraveled. "Er, feel like joining me in the sleeping bag?"

"Of course," she said. "And I need to ask you a question."

"What?"

"Are you really serious about chancing your arm in music?"

"Yes, I think I am. I know it seems ridiculous what with the fact that I've only been playing a full kit of drums for two years. But the music scene's changing. You don't have to be John Bonham to play bloody drums in a punk band."

"So you'll be working all kinds of fucking useless temp jobs and living in a squat, I suppose? Is there really a future in this?"

"I've no idea."

"But," she spluttered, "you don't even have any connections."

"I do now," I said. "I went up to town with Andy last week and met a couple of friends of his at the apparently rather fucking grand Royal College of Art. Out at the forefront of British design and all that. Very fucking elite. And two of these geniuses and some bird called Marion—they seem pretty nice—are putting a band together."

"Does it have a name?"

"Of course it bloody does. When was the last time you heard of a band that didn't have a name?"

"I'm listening."

"Hmmm. Well. If you must know. They're calling themselves the Art Attacks."

"That's fucking stupid."

"I knew you'd be impressed."

"I just don't believe this."

"You'll have to. Anyway. The Art Attacks you hate so much already, I think they're okay. Steve makes fucking amazing furniture—bit like Charles Eames—and his own guitars. And Ed draws peculiar cartoons. Marion wanks around in theater and stuff."

"I see," said Helen.

"And—I passed the audition."

"Really? So are they any good?"

"Hmmm," I said. "I'm not entirely sure that 'good' and 'bad' are much of an issue at this level."

"Oh, that sounds promising," Helen sniffed proudly. "You know, this isn't what I was expecting."

"Oh really? What were you expecting?"

"Something a bit less eccentric," she said. "I'm using my qualifications, and I was hoping you might use yours."

"Listen," I said, "I went to university on automatic bloody fucking pilot. 'Your future written in the best Parian marble money can buy,' signed, or should I say chiseled, 'N. Feather-stone.' Get your O's, get your A's, maybe even an S Level if you're a really clever bastard or a pathological swot, and, bingo, on to university."

"So your mind's made up?" said Helen. "And obviously has been for some time? Why didn't you tell me sooner?"

"Why didn't you argue about it sooner?"

"I think I was scared to."

"That makes two of us," I replied. "I saw this coming a mile off and I've been worried to bloody death about it. I knew you'd be upset. And I know your mum and dad won't be too pleased. Which is not to suggest that they wouldn't be fucking appalled if we ever got married, of course." (We had discussed marriage at times.)

"That's not true."

"I think it is," I said. "Don't get me wrong, Helen, I do happen to like them. They've always been nice to me. Very nice. But I don't think they trust me. And maybe they shouldn't."

"This is ridiculous."

"Is it?" I asked. "Is it? Your mum and dad can spot the yokel. The boozer in the bush hat, the B.A. with honors that means fuck-all because somewhere inside him, or so they imagine, he harbors allegiance to the East End's worst armpits and arseholes."

"If I could scream," she said, "I would, but your mum and dad have had quite enough awfulness for one day, John. And all *my* parents know about yours, if you must know, is that your dad's a communications engineer. Which is about as much as you know about my dad. What he does. For a living. Which isn't important."

"Maybe it's not," I conceded. "I'm sorry."

"What *is* important," she went on, "is that I love you. Even when you're being completely impossible. A handful. And, quite frankly, a nuisance. On our European trips. When you dress like a tramp and I have to leave you outside while I take a look at the hotels and pensions to see if they've got a room—because we'd never bloody get one if they saw you coming first."

This was true.

"So where do we go from here?" I asked. "Do you still love me?"

"Of course," she replied, but not before she'd punched me in the chest a good deal less than playfully. "But I really must do something to piss you off in return."

"Such as?"

"I know," said Helen, whose intimacies, at their most impetuous, had the *aigre-doux* flavor and tongue-twisting scent of the shadowy black olives on which we'd subsisted in Arles for eight days and Avignon for five in the summer of '74. "I'm not going to sit on your face again for at least a couple of weeks."

The relationship lasted another two years.

. . . .

a splat or two of all-devouring mustard

Joy at the commune, 1979

CHAPTER 10

Damage from Oily Chickpeas

. . . .

NINE MONTHS AFTER JOY'S WEDDING, ANDY PALMER FLEW TO
Phoenix, ostensibly simply to visit Joy (she was, as she had
told him, miserable) but actually to abduct her in the nicest
possible way. Barney, it seemed, had decided to replace what
little interest he'd ever had in sex with a morbid attachment to
yoga. Upon returning to England, Joy and Andy moved to a
meat-free commune superintended by the argumentative
health-food fanatic who had been so impolite about my wedding speech.

There they became significant ghosts—Joy sang; Andy
gave poorly tuned guitars a revolutionary pasting—in the
fervid machine known as Crass, perhaps the most radical
punk band that ever existed. A ferocious ensemble that made
Black Flag look like the Daughters of the American Revolu-
tion, they survived several visits from the secret police (who,
providentially, never said no to a nice cup of tea and a bis-

cuit), enjoyed an ethereal connection to the Sugarcubes and Björk, and earned my undying respect by ensnaring one of the many LPs they recorded—none of which I found listenable—in a photomontage whose agitatory nucleus was a bare-arsed Margaret Thatcher with several yards of sausages pouring from her rectum.

IN SEPTEMBER OF 1977, I moved to a squat in Brixton—back then, one of London's poorest and most derelict areas—that had been rendered habitable by two friends of Andy's: Alan, a painter (also a tireless creator of snippets of film seasoned with soft spots for Cartier-Bresson and Duchamp), and Ken, a dolorous conceptual artist from Manchester whose favorite bar was a hole in the ground (near Piccadilly Circus) patronized by Irish mutes who had perfected a method of sinking Guinness without ever stopping to breathe. There, I grew accustomed to a low-rent life of Chinese takeout, cigarette rationing, minimally remunerative gigs (except when we were fortunate enough to open for acts like Generation X, 999, and Wire), and a lack of hot water and heating.

In October, my parents' divorce became final, and the following month Dad withdrew from the dinghy he had doted on for twenty-one years, cramming the boot of his third-hand Ford Capri with a decade's worth of personal papers, a trash bag packed with slip-on shoes and shapeless casual trousers, a few treasured books (*Three Men in a Boat, From Here to Eternity,* Sir Charles Firth's biography of Cromwell, Uris's *Mila-18*), a carton of madly scratched LPs (*Seven Brides for Seven*

Brothers, Offenbach's *Tales of Hoffmann,* Copland's *Rodeo,* Beethoven's Fifth, Schubert's *Schwanengesang*). He also kept a single suit fit for a pointless wedding and two or three others that seemed appropriate for semi-silent Saturdays of fish and chips (dished up with dirt-cheap Riesling) at the Woodford Avenue maisonette that Jackie had moved to after Grandpa died. He then sadly set sail for a chintzy flat on Mornington Road, an undistinguished thoroughfare in Romford. The flat's owner was a sometime colleague, Angelika, a German woman who had moved to The Hague to marry a Dutchman who dabbled in plowshares and petrol.

Shortly thereafter, London fell foul of a cold spell so heinous it left me no choice but to click, clatter, chink, bang, and wallop along—when practicing with headphones at home—to the Buzzcocks, the Stooges, the Damned, the Dictators, Jonathan Richman, Patti Smith, and Abba while cocooned in Grandpa's terminal topcoat, a black look in virtually bulletproof wool that he'd snatched from a rack at a "toffee-nosed shop" just a tap dance away from St. Paul's. And one crestfallen Friday in the frosted middle distance of this tour de force of unrestrained inclemency, Geoffrey Jennings—a maladjusted roadie we'd bought for a fiver and the promise of a free plowman's lunch and a couple of pints of Tennent's—sullenly transported Alan, Ed, Steve, Marion, Ken, and me to Ongar, where Mum was still living while working in town as a secretary at the University of London's Institute of Education. Our mission was to pick up the family piano, which Marion was procuring for what Dad wryly called "the unimpressive sum of nothing" for her boyfriend, Rick, who played drums (very well) for the Motors.

—

STILL IN A STUPOR from fainting (in public) from what I suppose was partial starvation earlier in the day (as, too, had suspected the laughing policeman who helped me back onto my
feet) and pleading the need for an endmost review of the ill-
favored edifice where Mum and Dad had failed to settle their
differences, I told my companions, once the piano had been
loaded onto the van, that I would meet them down at the
Cock in about an hour.

I then took a farewell tour of the bricks, boards, and mor-
tar within whose twice-mortgaged embrace I had skipped,
shivered, skulked, glowered, laughed at Bob Hope, eagerly
waited for a visiting Grandpa to sing the Popeye song and to
drawl in East River overtones of Port Tewfik and Buffalo Bill
(whose circus he'd seen), and gristle and bone where men had
been, and lice.

I drifted from bedroom to bedroom and bathroom and
hallway to kitchen and lounge and, last, to the dining room.
On the sideboard, Mum (who moved out a week later) had
heaped my school reports: "Working well" (second-year
Latin); "Gets quite carried away at times" (third- and fourth-
form English composition); "Vocabulary good, translation
fair, grammar unacceptably erratic" (lower sixth Greek);
"Takes no interest" (first-form geography); "Team sports
seem not to be his strong point" (seven lamentable years of
involuntary submission to the mental defectives in charge of
all tennis and sprinting).

In a shopping bag, my postcards from Italy: "Dear Dad:
None of us like the spaghetti here but the meat sauce it comes
with is nice. Mussolini jokes have been discouraged" (partly

obscured by perspiration, Modena); "Dear Mum: I really loved 'Madonna of the Goldfinch.' Thank you again for the camera" (no spillage of any kind; *pasticceria* near the Uffizi); "Had a game of footer with some Italian paratroops. Lost by infinity to nothing. One of the prefects almost fell off the tower" (supremely cramped handwriting, minor damage from oily chickpeas; within sight of Pisa); "The wine from this region is said to be nice but we're not allowed to have any" (scripted aboard coach, further transfigured by Pepsi; Orvieto); "The most interesting frescoes are apparently out of bounds" (childish hand, one corner warped by contact with barely manageable slice of pizza; small town south of Pompeii).

In a separate envelope, a pittance of postcards from France: "Dear Mum and Dad: The weather is good. Chartres was fantastic. Hello to Joy. Love, John" (nightfall, day two); "I don't like the public toilets here" (morning, day three); "I had some wine called Sancerre. I hope you don't mind. Mr. Burgess says it's very good for you."

I walked to the window and gaped at the garden now stripped of flowers, its compost heap evicted. I sensed not just a recurring insufficiency of gratitude on my part but also a well-fed, reasonably well-read childhood here, now, belatedly ending. And just for a moment, the sense of exclusion, the sense of eternal estrangement, I'd felt upon first hearing the story of Dad's arrival at the orphanage overwhelmed me.

ON JANUARY 8, 1978, a few weeks after the Art Attacks' farewell performance—in which "Twist and Shout," our third and final encore, was given the Ramones treatment (by being played ridiculously fast), the Gary Glitter treatment (courtesy of the addition of a second drummer, Marion's boyfriend), and something not much resembling the *Playboy* treatment by dint of our having been joined onstage, in the opening bars, by an uninvited and none too attractive stripper—I attended my first rehearsal with a band called the Monochrome Set, whose primary influences, in a nutshell, were the Velvet Underground and Noël Coward.

This occasion of minimal import was staged in the bedroom belonging to the group's lead singer and songwriter, a salamander nicknamed Bid, whose mother (in an earlier incarnation, a jazz chanteuse) worked, coincidentally, in the same office as Mum. In recognition of the hunger that often attends life at the bottom of the musical *barrique*, she frequently punctuated our Saturday and Sunday practice sessions with (to my delight) lunches that reminded me of Ongar Primary dinners. (Bid's father, who was Indian and a published naturalist, toiled for the post office, worshipped cricket and the memory of Nehru, and, when doing none of those things, wrote poetry that I found reminiscent of Tagore.)

The ensemble's fortunes during the next four years were briskly summed up in a *Sounds* article about the British New Wave, written by Pete Frame and headed THE ART SCHOOL DANCE GOES ON FOREVER, that arrived at the newsstands on March 28, 1981: "Gigged sporadically and succeeded in alienating most thinking rock journalists. Are well aware of their minority appeal but see no barrier and intend to ride out whatever time it takes to break through." Our intermittent

and somewhat limited globe-trotting during our Rough
Trade and Dindisc (a Virgin subsidiary) signings took us first
throughout the United Kingdom, on a succession of peregri-
nations that included gigs—predictably poorly paid—in Halifax (where we stayed in a boardinghouse that had probably
changed very little since Engels had visited the town while re-
porting *The Condition of the English Working Class*); Derby
(where we had an engagement at the Ajanta, a not-quite-
derelict Indian cinema that reeked of vindaloo, and were
roused the following morning by what turned out to be, following a collective and terrified rush to the nearest window, a
Vulcan conducting a practice attack climb directly overhead);
Bristol (where, during a ten-minute trip to the zoo, an easily
offended tigress roared at our bass player so loudly that his
hands shook for hours); and Skegness (a seaside town in Lincolnshire where I saw the now long-vanished sight of retired
miners paddling in their suits).

Our two North American tours took us to the Northeast,
D.C., Toronto, Detroit, and the Upper Midwest. Our most
memorable dates—for me, this quality rarely had anything
to do with our reception—were in Chicago (where I sam-
pled my first kielbasa, dished up by a decrepit Pole with a
Salvador Dalí mustache), Milwaukee (where the sauerkraut
turned out to be ten times as good as the version once
served in London at a tourist trap called Schmidt's), Boston
(where, though utterly unfamiliar with clams, I quickly
came to appreciate the chowder), and New York. In the
space of the week and a half we spent playing in Manhattan
(at the Mudd Club, Hurrah, and Irving Plaza), Long Island,
and New Jersey, I acquired a taste for banana cream pie (at

Howard Johnson's), White Castle cheese fries, most things on the menu at Burger King, embryonic New York sushi (at Taste of Tokyo), and, thanks to a musty concatenation of secondhand stores dispensing books and records, John Dos Passos, Herman Melville, Wallace Stevens, James Agee, William Saroyan, Johnny Cash, Thelonious Monk, Bill Evans, and Sonny Rollins.

It was also during our first American tour that I met an incredibly gentle and good-humored young woman from the Midwest named Pam, an aspiring jewelry designer and also a fabulous cook, whose gravlax, polenta, and rosemary chicken remain, to this day, the best I've ever tasted. She had moved to New York after graduating (with a B.F.A.) from Washington University, in St. Louis, where she'd been born.

Following my return to London from the first American tour, in '79, Pam and I began to correspond regularly. By the middle of '81, when the Monochrome Set's finances had become so precarious that the dinner I had in Paris en route home from an Italian expedition consisted of a single glass of water and a mouthful of nettles on permanent loan from Bid, we were in love and had decided that I should find more profitable employment and begin to save enough money to move to New York. For the next six months, I worked in a Casio warehouse in Clerkenwell.

I also began to see a good deal more of Mum, who was now living in London and dating a retired (and demonstrably middle-class) professor of industrial design named Roger Bennett. Roger, to my unvoiced disgust, had not only been a conscientious objector during the war but had also, back in the '60s, done some consulting (with regard, I believe, to their light show) for the band that produced (thanks to Syd Barrett) a single (in my opinion) creditable 45 ("See Emily Play") and (without Barrett) three of my least favorite albums: *Meddle, The Wall,* and *Dark Side of the Moon.*

Mum's culture campaign, in which I suspect she had never felt entirely victorious, now resumed—and I appreciated it a good deal more than I had in a previous eon. By December 1981, we had accompanied each other to a number of exceptional concerts by the London Symphony Orchestra at the Royal Festival and Royal Albert halls: *Carmina Burana* and Chávez's *Horse Power Suite* (conducted by the late Eduardo Mata, whose Cuban heels, extreme good looks, and astonishingly elegant suit particularly caught Mum's attention); Brahms's Violin Concerto and Ravel's *Daphnis et Chloé* (the former with Perlman as soloist, both pieces chillingly overmastered by Previn); and an overpowering reading, by Abbado, of Giuseppe Verdi's *Requiem.*

At the National Theatre, we caught a Royal Shakespeare Company production of two plays by Schnitzler; at the National Film Theatre and elsewhere, some retrospectives—Cassavetes, De Sica, and Bergman—and, for the fourth time, my favorite Jack Lemmon film, *Save the Tiger.* And on the last Saturday before Christmas we found ourselves comprising roughly a quarter of the audience at an afternoon screening, in a cinema on Oxford Street, of Joseph Losey's *Don Giovanni.* This masterpiece provoked an interest in opera that I was not to relinquish until the last of my operagoing friends in New York, all of whom were gay, died of AIDS in the mid-1990s.

With Mum and Joy, January 1982

"That was marvelous," said Mum as we were shown to a table at a Pizza Express. "I've got goose bumps."

"You're not the only one," I croaked, extracting a cigarette. "That bit where the poor bugger got his comeuppance was terrifying. The music rather matched the mood, I must say. Remind me to look up the definition of *commendatore* sometime. And, by the way, you're looking really good these days. Something to do with Roger?"

"I suppose so, dear," she replied, a little flustered but not too embarrassed.

And about time, too, I thought to myself. Joy and I had a theory that she and Dad had never had sex again after Joy was conceived. It must be quite nice, I conjectured, to be getting some again after a dry spell like that.

"I'm sorry I won't be here for the wedding," I said. (I'd

booked a nonrefundable one-way ticket to New York a month before Mum and Roger had made the announcement.)

"Oh, that's okay, dear. These things happen. Can't be helped. What color wine do you want?"

"Oh. Er—white. Thank you."

"What about the pizza?"

"Onion, anchovy, olives. Always used to have that here. When I was at college. Lunch every Friday after my Greek Religion class. Special subject—wasn't offered at RHC so I had to come up to London for it."

Mum continued: "Er—you and Pam—you will be getting married, won't you? She's ever so nice."

"I know she is. And, yes, we will be getting married. And not just because it gets me a green card."

"A what?"

"Green card. Work permit. Resident alien status."

"I hope you'll be happy," she said slightly sadly.

"So do I. And I'm sure we will. And I hope it all goes well for you and Roger."

"Thank you," she said. "Could I have a cigarette?"

"Of course," I said, handing her the packet. "Sorry it's not a Gitane. You'll have to make do with a Camel."

"Joseph Losey—you know he directed *King and Country*, don't you?"

"Of course I do," I said, remembering how peeved I'd been at being too young to see the film at the time of its general release. "We watched it on telly at 207 after Grandpa died, and you made a point of pointing that out. God, that seems such a long time ago now. Remember that scene with the firing squad? Up with the guns—all set to let fly—and the poor bloody sods with a conscience are suddenly aiming to miss."

"It was heartbreaking, absolutely heartbreaking. The three of us went to see it when it first came out."

"The three of us?"

"Me and Jackie and Grandpa. I wished we hadn't, afterwards."

"Why?"

"Because it was too much for Dad. He almost threw up. When Dirk Bogarde gave Tom Courtenay the coup de grâce."

"Oh, yes—the single shot to the head," I said. "God, that was a terrible sequence. It was raining, wasn't it? In the film. Absolutely pissing."

"Yes," said Mum. "I sometimes think it reminded Dad of

In Brixton, 1981

the day his best friend, Charlie, got the chop. You know—the whizz-bang. Or something like that."

"The bloke with *no* head. That wouldn't surprise me."

"They were up to their waists in water when that happened."

"I know—you told me."

ON FEBRUARY 13, 1982, Dad drove me and my portable goods (a cigarette lighter, a Casio watch, two packets of Embassy, a comb, an electric razor, secondhand copies of Siegfried Sassoon's *Memoirs of an Infantry Officer* and William Golding's *The Spire,* and a cheap suitcase bulging with touring-tattered underwear and outerwear and a boxed set of symphonies by Brahms) to Heathrow. We were accompanied by Jackie, who wanted to treat us to lunch once I'd checked in. Dad had been a little dismayed, at first, to learn that I was planning to move to the United States, and he was far less talkative than usual. So was Jackie, who, now that I thought about it, had been doting on me in her own way for almost twenty-eight years.

"Well, son," said Dad, inspecting the menu with very little interest, "I know you're off to get hitched and all that, and Pam's ever so nice. But, well—I'm sorry you're leaving. Hope you don't mind my saying so."

"Of course not, Dad. I understand. But this is the way it has to be. Pam and I are in love. And she doesn't want to move here. And, I mean, I'm not disappearing forever. I'll be coming back whenever I can."

(Which may not be too often, I thought, given this family's track record where money's concerned.)

"I'm sure you will," said Dad, lighting up a Woodbine. "But it feels strange. Do you think you'll miss England? I know I've asked you that before, but still . . . I wonder. Isn't New York a bit dangerous? I know you've been there twice now. . . ."

"I'll be careful, believe me," I said. "And Pam knows the place inside out. And of course I'll miss England. A lot."

"Still," said Dad, "I'm sure you'll find it interesting. America, I mean. Not just New York. And very different. Seems to me that class isn't quite as much of an issue over there."

"That's what Daddy always said," interjected Jackie. "He would have stayed if Mummy could have coped with the weather."

"I've heard that, too," I said, in a tone of voice designed to disguise my skepticism. "About class, that is. We'll see."

I would now consider the meal abominable—overcooked sole in a sauce that smelled a bit like rotten oranges, followed by apple pie with an integument approximating bone—but it was something of a culinary success by Ongar, Brixton, Romford, and Redbridge standards, and by the time it was over, both Dad and Jackie seemed to be in a slightly better mood. To my regret, though—a regret that pained me in an instant then and hurts today whenever the memory recurs—the happier frame of mind failed to last. As soon as we arrived at the gate to the departure lounge, Jackie began to snivel. Dad, whom I had only ever seen crying once before, kept better control of himself but nevertheless ended up emptying his nose several times into a typically crustacean handkerchief.

"Oh God," I said, "I'm sorry. I'll be back. As often as possible—I promise. For God's sake, Dad, I was born here."

"Well," said Dad, now dabbing at his eyes. "Promise me you'll never forget that."

AS THE KUWAIT Airways Boeing 747 stumbled aloft and slowly began to turn its tail on Europe, I stared down amid hopes and misgivings—and a dim appreciation of the risk involved in moving so very far away for something as unreliable, as mutable, as love—at the pleasantries and greenness of the island containing an island I still thought of as possibly, just possibly, my true home.

At the same time (I was thinking through Jackie to Grandpa), nothing, even now, spoke to me with more force of my country than visions of hundreds of thousands of British soldiers fighting and dying in holes in the ground in France. Imagined puffs of pitch-black smoke and runnels of blood in a mire still obscured—an Iraqi flight attendant quietly, with immense reserve, said "Soda?"—the less compelling apparitions that were also crowding around me.

Two adults and two children attacking roast lamb in a dining room the size of a Ping-Pong table in a house in a village a few miles to the north of the Thames, in a distant and bellicose year. Suddenly, aircraft overhead—fast, low, black-hearted, all skulls-and-crossbows, and (oh, how my sister screamed) loud. The adults are exchanging nervous glances. Dogs bark; Twinkle scarpers, saucer of water sent arse over tit, every ounce of fur on petrified end. "What's wrong, Mum?" I remember saying. "Nothing, darling—and please

don't eat so fast, John, it's not good for you." "What's for afters?" "Banana custard, if you must know." "Ooh, good."
(Another of Dad's elementary specialties.) "I was going to
bake some apples but they'd all gone wormy." (Good job, too,
I thought to myself. I hate baked apples.) "Oh," I said. "Dad,
where's Cuba?"

Mum again, half an hour earlier, a silhouette against the
kitchen window, crying—wishing she hadn't married Dad?
or simply afraid of expiring in a flash?—while rewarding
the humble cabbage with a muscular addition of insult to in-
jury in the form of a method of straining that perhaps still
stands as most peculiar ever contrived, pinning down the
dead leaves at the bottom of the saucepan with a potato
masher, rotating the pan ninety degrees, and frantically
squashing the helpless comestible, now denuded of its vitamin content, until it had shed enough water to be capable of
squatting on a plate with consummate grace and no abound-
ing puddle.

ONCE OVER GREENLAND, I felt a new world beginning to
beckon with absolute finality, a new world of which I knew
little but Pam, who would be meeting me at Kennedy and
whose dad, a Winstons-and-whiskey addict named Russ, had
expired, when she was twenty-six, of cancer of the lung. She
sometimes thought he had never fully recovered from the two
years he spent in prison camps following his descent from a
crippled B-24 just minutes away from unloading its bombs
onto Frankfurt.

And then, as Boston fell astern, I found myself (illogically) thinking—when not buried alive in Sassoon—of classics department coffee mornings at college, hosted by our resident reader in Latin, a vivacious Scottish lesbian who also knew a great deal about New Comedy.

I suddenly felt, not quite completely, lost.

CHAPTER 11

The Graying Purveyors
of Haddock and Eels

. . . .

THE FIRST OF THE NINE YEARS THAT PAM AND I SPENT LIVING
in her studio apartment on Fifteenth Street in Chelsea (before
moving to Brooklyn in 1991) witnessed my removal from the
musical sphere to the slightly more remunerative milieu of
publishing, the profession to which—given my temperament,
my intellectual foibles, and, I can now see, the lasting effects
of the culture campaign—I appeared to be most suited. Pam,
for her part, persisted with her jewelry and was eventually
able to move her business out of our home and into a minuscule office in a commercial building on Union Square. We
made the most of whatever the city had to offer that involved
very little expense, and duly became habitués of Central Park,
Prospect Park, and the major museums.

My father's comments on the subject of class in America
soon began to ring a little hollow. I found the distinctions less
overt than in England but existent nonetheless, and thought it

unsurprising that I had married a woman whose background was much like my own.

BETWEEN 1982 AND 1998, my return trips to Britain were, largely for reasons of economy, few and far between, which, in turn, forced me to follow my family's fortunes from a distance. Joan (her liver, like Dick's, in ruins) died in 1983, six months after her spouse. Ena passed away in a nursing home in 1990, Eileen (unexpectedly, and also of heart failure) shortly after a minor operation in 1994. Don (who had had a brush with lung cancer, which went into remission with treatment, that same year) and Rose continued to reside on the Isle of Dogs even though, with the advent of the efflorescence of glass and steel known as Canary Wharf and the near simultaneous demise of the docks, the physical and economic contortions of the once solidly working-class enclave where they'd lived since getting married were changing beyond recognition. Joy left the commune in 1987 with her new partner, Pip (a fellow communitarian), and moved to London, while Aunt Jackie remained in her tidy maisonette, where she was visited every Saturday evening by Dad, whose health began to fail in 1991 with the onset of obstructive airways disease.

The most momentous event during this period, however—from my point of view and from Joy's—was the death of my mother's second husband, in 1988. The marriage had begun to collapse almost as soon as the honeymoon was over. This, according to Joy, had resulted in six years' worth of rancor being acted out on the unforgiving stage of Roger's forbiddingly bargelike, vaguely Danish Modern, eco-friendly single-story house in a village in Norfolk. His estate was divided between Mum and his children from a previous marriage, and in 1991, Mum, having completely depleted what was only a very modest inheritance, reached retirement age with no means of support in prospect other than the basic old-age pension. She then applied for assistance to the local authorities and was placed in a drafty and prone-to-damp flat in a sheltered-housing facility in Norwich.

She was, to all intents and purposes, almost as poor as Nana Haney had been, which—allied with the fact that secondhand memories of penury had been haunting me since childhood to such an extent that, with the passage of time, I'd come increasingly to suspect that no amount of good fortune or happiness could ever serve to moderate their potency, let alone erase them altogether—left me feeling both embarrassed and ashamed, not least because it had never occurred to me that something close to pennilessness would ever be repeated in my family. Mum's lifelong looking up, the ambitions she had nurtured since her teens, had let her down. Middle-class Roger, once off the leash of mere romance and settled in the marriage, had, she said, turned out to be demanding, unreasonable, and—at times—a snob.

Mum's circumstantial reduction gradually resulted in a measure of depression that Joy did her best to alleviate by providing her with as much emotional support as she possibly could—which, given the fact of their geographical separation, was far from easy. Mum, whose stubborn streak didn't always serve her well, refused to move to London to be near Joy, so my sister had to supplement the emotional support with visits to Norwich to clean house for Mum (who, because of her dejection and her contempt for housework, had few qualms about living in a pigsty) and to top up what little money she had. (Mum, true to form, still found buying books infinitely more satisfying than staying on top of her bills.) The predicament placed an immense strain on my sister and Pip until 2005, when a singularly gifted social worker discovered that Mum had not been receiving all the benefits to which she was entitled. As a result, Mum was to be a good deal happier in the last few months of her life than she had been for the previous fourteen years.

UNCLE DAVE, THE PATRIARCH of Dad's generation of the family, passed away in his sleep in the autumn of 1996. Despite the departures of Eileen, Ena, Dick, and Joan, it was not until

With Mum and Joy, 1989

this death that I first sensed the true commencement of the dissolution not only of the Haney side of my clan but also of a measure of the sense of security (and identity) that I had always derived from being a part of it.

On the morning after Dave's funeral, which I couldn't attend, Joy called not only to bemoan his exit once more but also to affectionately note that the buffet dished up by Pauline had been less than vegetarian friendly—a ramekin of mustard, a slapdash platter of silverside and tongue, some hastily made ham rolls, trace amounts of greenery, a pork pie the size of a birthday cake, orange juice, soda, and beer.

"Sounds good to me," I instinctively blurted. "Pork without end, and the talkative part of a cow. I'm so jealous."

"I'm sure you are," said Joy. "And I'm not being critical. It's just that I've been so out of touch. With Dad's side of the

Dad and Uncle Dave, 1991

family. I seem to forget—between weddings and funerals—
that they probably think of me as the fusspot. The one with
the really weird diet."

"I really doubt that," I said. "Don't be so hard on yourself."

"I'm not being hard on myself," she snapped. "I'm
being . . . realistic."

"You're not being remotely realistic, believe me. Have
any of them ever been unkind to you?"

"Of course they haven't."

"There you are, then."

"I still think they don't approve of me."

"Why?"

"Oh—I don't know. Why should they approve of me?
Only eats vegetables. Lived on a commune. Bit of an anar-
chist, too, Uncle Den says."

"I think you're way off the mark here," I said.

"Well, I'm sorry, I still think you're wrong. You do realize, don't you, that the last time I'd seen them until the other
day was when I got married."

"So? What's twenty years between friends?"

"A long time, quite frankly," said Joy. "They don't know
what to make of me, John. How on earth could they? They're
so working-class. Living it up down Memory Lane. Everyone
sticking together, and stuck in a rut. You know the code
here—labels, divisions, upper, middle, (bloody) lower, left a
bit, right a bit, everyone measuring everyone else and sum-
ming each other up."

"Of course I know the fucking code. You grow up with
that crap, you never forget. It begins in the bloody bootees,
quite frankly—and it's still going strong on the bedpan."

"So I don't play that game anymore. Well, I try not to. But. Sometimes I feel a bit sad—believe it or not—not belonging."

"You really think you don't belong?" I sputtered, beginning to feel more than a little annoyed with her. "Pull the other one. You're as working-class as the rest of us. And you're stuck with it, for fuck's sake. Just as much as they are. You can't see it off with celery root, you know. And I don't think they're so stuck, either. It's not as if they're sitting around wishing they were back in bloody Plaistow."

"I suppose not," said Joy.

"But they haven't forgotten where they came from, and why the hell should they?"

"Getting back to the celery root," said Joy. "That's a bit of a joke, if you ask me, coming from someone who works at *Saveur,* loves foie gras, and never says no to a glass of champagne."

"It's the diplomatic me. My cosmopolitan side. Sheer pretense. Smoke and mirrors. Solely for consumption over here."

"Rubbish."

"It's true," I huffed. "Kick me out of a cab on Mornington Road and I'll probably end up buying a copy of the *Beano* and asking Dad if he's got any fish sticks or cannonball peas in the house."

"Dad never touches fish fingers," said Joy. "He can't stand them."

"That's not the point," I snapped. "I'm talking about my *basic* preferences."

"They're not written in stone," said Joy. "Your tastes in other things have changed."

With Joy, 1990

"Maybe so," I said. "Maybe so—but it's different with food."

AT THE END OF OCTOBER 1998, his lungs and his laughter locked solid by rot, his spouse at his side and sympathetic nurses in attendance, Uncle Don lost his long battle with a second bout of lung cancer—a day before I was due to fly to England for a visit. (Pam was joining me a few days later.)

By the time the brand-new Boeing had bounced and thudded, alarmingly hard, onto the runway at Heathrow, I had read most of *Endymion* while listening to *Der Rosenkavalier*, ingested too much Diet Coke for dangerously elevated comfort, begun to wonder whether the Internet bubble wasn't about to burst, and also commenced sporadic speculation as to what (apart from sherry, stout, and tea) Rose might be planning for the menu at the wake. Pickled onions, perhaps. Cocktail wieners, possibly. A sausage roll or six. Stairways of silverside. Hillocks of ham—and, thus, fluorescent lagoons of piccalilli.

This contemplation produced a decision to beg Pip and Joy, who were picking me up, for permission to visit the nearest airport eating establishment serving the kind of low-rent food that Pam so dreads.

"So," I asked, clumsily shunting an offcut of brittle fried bread—akin to the plywood I'd guzzled with glee at St. Mawgan and Binbrook and Coningsby—into the core of an undercooked yolk and recalling both how good and, at the same time in this instance, how productive of a certain cheerlessness my first sniff of English air in three years, just a few minutes earlier, had been. "How's Dad taking it?"

"Philosophically, of course," said Joy, averting her gaze as I scooped up a lump of blood pudding. "Better than he did when Dave went. So far."

"Really?" I mused, eagerly dissecting the bigger of two bangers so runty that Dad would never have allowed them into the house. "I suppose that makes sense. Dave was always standing in for David Haney, Senior. He did it very well. Dick, Dad, Don, Ray—they all looked up to him."

"I sometimes think they worshipped him," Joy coughed and cringed as I seamlessly shoveled cruds of meat into a bog of baked beans.

"Can't say I blame them," I slurped. "Good bloke, Dave. And that's the only accolade that matters."

"And how are you taking it?"

"Hasn't really hit me yet—but, believe me, it will," I said, dreading the imminence of a fundamental upset I had by now begun to sense but had yet to fully feel. "Probably when we get there. To Don's place, I mean. I had one of the happiest evenings of my life on the Isle of Dogs."

"The Christmas party?" said Joy.

"Yes," I said. "Do you remember much about it?"

"Not really," said Joy. "Usual blur of beer and cigs. Cuddles from Rose and Eileen. Boozy kisses from Joan. Dressed up in one of those smart little frocks Mum always made me wear on special occasions. I was never allowed those nylon frills. Like the cousins. That made me jealous, you know."

"That particular blur of beer and cigs was the best bloody party I've been to," I said. "Right up there with the rest of what might be called, oh, I don't know, the emotional milestones. Of which there are just three others, if you count the assault-course contest. And, by the way, you weren't wearing a frock at that do. Mum had you stuffed in a pleated skirt and some lacy puff-sleeved blouse."

"And the milestones were . . . ?"

"You really want to know?" I asked. "One, bouncing up and down above Lincolnshire thanks to a bunch of jokers in a Vulcan. Two, going all the way with Helen for the very first time. Which also involved a certain amount of bouncing up and down."

"Yeah, yeah," said Joy, yawning.

"I know," I said. "I'm being crude. But it's second nature now and always has been. Three, Don's party. And, last but not least, my moment of glory at the North Weald Air Show."

"Interesting selection," said Joy. "And Don's is the only booze-up on the list. Was it really that good?"

"I thought so."

"And which was the best of all?"

"Don's do," I chirped without hesitation, glimpsing again, as I had many times and still do, the long-dead tins of Cydrax and the sight of my hands coated with ham fat, strawberry jam, and crisp crumbs.

"I'm sure it was," said Joy, having first inserted a fry into the deeps of yet another yawn. "And so much for sentiment."

"What do you mean?"

"Your nostalgia for the Cold War. It's over."

"More or less," I said, tastelessly dropping a dying Camel into the dregs of my tea. "And absolutely no bloody thanks to the 'Ban the Bomb' contingent."

Joy rolled her eyes.

"And, yes, it is strange," I continued. "It's totally perverse. Maybe we should chalk it up to *Valiant* and *Victor*."

"Mum wouldn't argue with that."

"No," I said. "She wouldn't. And thank you for indulging my desperate need for a plateload of out-and-out garbage. The chips were particularly awful. Maybe I should ask if they were yesterday's reheated. Whatever. And by the way—how is she? Wasn't sounding all that good the last bloody time I talked to her."

"Pretty depressed," said Joy. "And disorganized. I'm helping her with her bills these days. If you must know."

"Oh," I said. "I thought she was more or less making ends meet."

"Well, she's not. In fact, I've been meaning to ask if you could chip in, too."

"I wish you'd asked me sooner."

"She's had her phone cut off three times now, I'm afraid."

"Doesn't surprise me. Dad was always tearing his fucking hair out over the phone bills at Number 13."

"And she's in a mess with her rent."

"I see. So what's it going to take?"

"Sixty quid a month would cover half of it."

THE UNMAPPED JOURNEY to Joy's abode took the scenic route along the north bank of the Thames, embracing wet views of Westminster Abbey, the Tate, and the Festival Hall. When we arrived in Crystal Palace, I grudgingly consented to chamomile tea but eventually demanded an enormous glass of Cloudy Bay sauvignon blanc. I then trudged upstairs with the bottle and slowly unpacked in a guest room overcome by unshelved books, among them some that I suddenly realized I must have left behind in 1982: *If This Is a Man*, *The Last of the Just*, *The Charterhouse of Parma*, and *The Plague*.

"Any more books of mine lying around?" I asked when Joy came in to say goodnight.

"Probably," she said. "Not really sure. We only unboxed this lot the other week."

"Well, do let me know what you do dig up," I sniffed, suddenly noting that two or three tears had now become one with my wine.

"Are you okay?"

"Not really," I said. "It's been a long time, hasn't it? I mean, since I moved to the States."

"Er . . . yes," said Joy. "But I don't remember you bringing it up before. Well, not often."

"It's different now. Oh, God, why do I suddenly *really* feel like shit?"

"You do?"

"Yes. I do. You know what? It's losing Don. It's tipped some kind of balance. He was the only one who stayed. Slap bloody bang in the center. Ciggie in the middle. Four-fucking-square on the Isle of Dogs. And this coming Thursday I'll be back there for only the fourth time in thirty-nine years. And the last time was—what?—seventeen years ago. Cousin Diane's engagement party. In a pub, where else? Near the water. Dad and I went for an hour. And that was when Don got stuck in with such a bloody odd question."

"Really?"

"Yeah. He wandered over when Dad was off having a piss. And he asked me if I thought I was better than them. (What with me being the only bloke with a bloody degree in the family.) Better than him. And Rosie. And the girls. And his mates and his neighbors. I couldn't believe that fucking bee was buzzing around in his bonnet. Saddest bloody question I've been asked."

"And the third time?" backtracked Joy, who had no recollection at all of Rose's sister's wedding.

"Rose and Don's twentieth wedding anniversary. You were in Arizona."

"Oh," said Joy. "So what did you say to Don?"

"No."

"Did he believe you?"

"Eventually."

"Did you tell Dad?"

"I decided not to. But I think he knew something was up. I kept pretty bloody quiet when he was driving me back to Brixton."

"So what was up . . . I mean . . . exactly?"

"Exactly? The distance between two words—I mean 'worlds'—I suppose. The hidden costs of a so-called education."

"Well, I'm sorry to have to say this, John," said Joy, "but that isn't exactly what I had. I only went to the Dump, you know. And got through a foundation course that led nowhere."

"Hold it right there," I said, pouring myself some more wine. "Let's forget the Eleven Plus. The O's. The A's. You got two, I got three. Doesn't seem worth fighting over. And let's forget, please, let's forget my degree. Let's talk about the leg-up."

"What leg-up?" said Joy.

"The leg-up, love," I clucked, spotting *Comet in Moominland* condensed between the carpet and *The Waves* and, at the same time, seeing Don smoking an Embassy and looking noncommittally at a table covered in quiche. "The leg-up without which I doubt we'd have done as well—okay, moderately well—as we have. The extracurricular stuff. Which really happened quite by chance, you know. Grapher and spouse with two tiny children and the East End written all over them—kind of—move to a semidetached in the country and wind up being virtually adopted by the local literati. Who happen to live next door."

"I suppose that was a stroke of luck," said Joy.

"That was unbelievable luck," I said, netting a fritillary and killing it scientifically (with chloroform) with Matthew in the Skiptons' back garden. "The Skiptons. Mr. Burgess. Jane. The Ramsays. Jennifer. Quite the collective kick, I'd say, all the way up the intellectual backside. Mum got a massive return on that fiver."

"What fiver?" said Joy.

"The deposit," I replied, remembering Mum's metallic exposition of the reasons for our not quite frenetically hurried defection to Ongar from Rainham. "On the house we grew up in."

"I suppose she did," said Joy. "But I still don't quite see what you're getting at. We were talking about Don ten minutes ago. And then you went off on this almost hysterical detour."

"Sorry about the amateur theatrics," I said, staring out the window in the direction of Kent, which was not to be seen, and thinking of departed Aunt Ena's dignity and reserve and of Joan projecting lemon slices into a gin and tonic. "But the detour and Don are related. What I'm trying to say is that none of this crap—what you know, what you've read, what you do, how much you make, whether or not you happen to know one bloody end of an olive from the other—is much of an issue where Don lives."

"You mean 'lived,' " said Joy. "And are you really sure about that? After all, he did ask that question."

"It's not the same," I said, suddenly wanting to cry for Don, to be in a pub on the Isle of Dogs and, in an otherwise empty corner, drinking alone but not necessarily slowly. "What I mean is, you don't get a grilling. It's all very live-and-let-live. Which is, I think, the essence of our other education."

"Meaning?"

"The sentimental one," I said, shivering atop York Minster with the Ramsays and Joy on an August afternoon in 1970 and holding on tight to a secondhand copy of a French edition of Propertius that Edward had just bought for me. "The stuff

Joy and Pip in Crystal Palace Park, 1998

that makes us—made us—you and me—what we are when what little brain we happen to have gets taken out of the equation. How did the kindness we're capable of—not too much in my case, of course—actually get to be there?"

"Thanks to Mum and Dad," said Joy. "Who else?"

"I know that," I said, seeing Dad, in the Austin—which smelled of puke, thanks to Joy, and mince pies—studiously peering through the windscreen at night in search of a readable sign for the Blackwall Tunnel. "But there was something about Don's Christmas do that hit me between the eyes. We were . . . I'm not quite sure how to put this. Back at the source? On Dad's side. I'd already had a taste of it at that wedding you can't remember. And, oh, a bit more when they trekked out to Ongar for fish paste and mountains of peanuts.

But Don's do. Don's do was different. The unbelievably tid-
dly house. The Thames a hundred yards away. The docks just
up the road. And the bomb sites. There were still a few of
those around in 1962."

"A few?" replied Joy. "There were loads."

"You know what?" I continued, forlornly and finally
mourning, in something like fullness, the loss of my childhood, too many foundational grown-ups, and my youth.
"Don's place—and I'm fucked if I know why—means as
much to me as Number 207. Which makes no sense at all. I
mean, Jesus, I've only ever been inside it once."

"It doesn't have to make any sense," said Joy.

"So how's Dad doing? Really?" I asked. "He always pre-
tends to be doing okay when I get him on the phone. 'Mustn't
complain.' 'Mustn't grumble.' 'Not too bad.' 'You know what
I always say, son? Cheer up, mate—there's always someone
much worse off than you.' There's no getting Dad down, is
there?"

"There is these days," said Joy. "He's not doing very well
at all. Much worse than the last time you were over, I'm
afraid. Now we've got more room, I've been thinking he
could live with us, if need be." (Joy and Pip had recently
moved from a tiny rented flat to a rented three-story house.)

FOLLOWING AN EXCURSION to Norwich—where, in return for
a huge piece of halibut she couldn't afford plus a pint of carrot soup, a Sainsbury's pork pie, a couple of bangers, and two
fried eggs, I took Mum out shopping for books, bric-a-brac,
and some winter-proof shoes—I arrived at Dad's apartment
at about five o'clock, to a dusting of snow, three days later. He

had the top floor and the attic of a two-story house like many others in Romford.

Letting myself in as quietly as possible in case he was having a snooze, I hauled my suitcase up the stairs and parked it next to an ineffective stool that he'd salvaged from Mayflower Way. Then, having left my outer layers on his almost useless coat stand, I tiptoed past the kitchen—which smelled, not unpleasantly, of cabbage—and into his lair, whose inanimate entrails at that time comprised a grumpy sofa, two armchairs from which the elderly could be extracted only with considerable force, a dining table far too big for the window bay into which it had been wedged, an aging TV, a CD player that neither Dad nor his roommate—a Graham Greene addict named Reg who worked at Reuters—ever used, a VCR, and a shaky bookshelf largely laden with twentieth-century history. On the mantelpiece sat two photographs featuring Joy, one a straightforward school portrait, the other of her and Sandy (at age thirteen) pulling faces with several other young women from the Dump on a school trip to London Zoo.

Dad was apparently fast asleep, his face madly haggard, more heavily lined, to my horror, than I had ever seen it before, his hair (still black despite his age) in total disarray, his skinny wrists protruding from the twisted sleeves of a regulation navy-blue and dandruff-scattered V-neck, his undusted spectacles and an unopened ounce of tobacco in his lap. Beside him, the surface of the table had all but disappeared beneath the landfill of his life's end: cigarette lighters, boxes of matches, a ruler, screwdrivers, pliers, a T-square, inhalers (both active and discarded), packets of codeine, Grampian ashtrays, outdated diaries, doctor's prescriptions, mobile

With Dad in Romford, 1998

phone, minuscule address book, nail scissors, corn plasters, cotton balls, chewed Biros, the nubs of numerous pencils, an empty box of Quality Street chocolates, and bread crumbs.

At which point, he opened his eyes.

"Ha-ha!" he said and then, gasping for breath, slowly began to heave himself out of his chair. "Had you fooled. Heard you coming a mile away. You sounded like a herd of elephants coming up those stairs."

"Don't get up, Dad," I said with unusual firmness, distraught at the sight he presented and trying not to show it. "You were looking so comfortable there."

"Comfortable?" he said, hobbling toward me. "Comfortable? You must be bloody joking. Horrible chair, that. And what do you mean, 'Don't get up'? How often do I see you?"

Having then hugged me harder than I had ever been hugged by anyone other than Pam—who had come close to crushing the life out of me at JFK in 1982—he said: "You're not looking too bad, mate. Fancy something to eat?"

"Only if it's no trouble," I replied, thinking, unaccountably, of Mum's fish pies (which, and I had no idea why, she stopped manufacturing when I was in my mid-teens) and then, more sensibly, suddenly wondering whether England would still feel like home once Mum, Dad, Jackie, Rose, and Ray were all gone.

"Of course it's no trouble. Let's see. There's some bubble and squeak left over from lunch. Reheat that. Sling in some bacon. That'll be nice. And I was thinking of opening a tin of soup for myself. Tomato. We can share it. And there's some apple pie from yesterday. So I'll take care of that lot and you can put the kettle on. How does that sound?"

"Just can't wait," I grinned in deceit, while feeling completely floored by the slowly but surely vanishing act in Stygian progress before me.

THIS, THEN, WAS the impromptu meal that set the tone for most of my intake during the week that ensued. Lunch the next day was a childhood Tuesday standard: sausages with onion gravy (a viscous slurry of lifeless onions and irrigated Bisto), mashed potatoes containing an infusion of butter that even Fernand Point might have found excessive, and a virtual Kilimanjaro of cannonball peas. The next day, Dad produced a dinner that always reminds me of childhood winter Sundays: chicken puffed up with a pound of butter, quartered potatoes roasted in the pan juices, carrot slices the size of silver dollars, and tepid broad beans as big as a bulldog's testicles. Tea (eggs, bacon, baked beans, and a slice of two-day-old bread pudding with a bottom crust the consistency of cardboard) followed barely two hours later. And on the day before Don's funeral, I treated Dad to lunch at the Mornington Arms, the terminally unremarkable pub a few steps down the road.

"Anything in particular worth eating here?" I asked, scanning the menu and contentedly wallowing in the almost monkish silence that overruns some (but not all) pubs in the London suburbs at lunchtime on a weekday.

"Well, it's not the Black Bass," said Dad, referring to an upscale restaurant in Lumberville, Pennsylvania, where Pam and I had treated him, in 1991, when her business was having a good year, to what was almost certainly the most expensive meal he ever savaged: superior shellfish, rack of lamb, apricot galette, three kinds of stink-bomb fromage (which he actually liked), and some decent Chablis. "It's a pub. In case you hadn't noticed. In Romford. But the steak, chips, and peas are okay."

"I'm sure they are, mate," I said. "You'd have to go some to fuck that up."

The steak, when it came, was as stiff as a board, the chips brunette, the peas fatigued, the gravy lukewarm.

"Hmmm," I said. "I guess I was wrong. Someone's fucked up really badly here. It's a good job I'm bloody well starving."

"Some things never change, do they?"

"What do you mean?"

"You," he replied. "Liking your nosh. I think I must have begun calling you Hungry Horace when you were ever so tiny. Still, at least you aren't a messy eater these days."

"Joy had an appetite, too," I retorted. "And she still does.

You should take it as a compliment, mate. You and Mum were wonderful cooks. And you still are. And I'm sorry if my mode of ingestion seemed indelicate at times."

"Indelicate?" said Dad. "It was worse than that. Particularly where meat was concerned. You know, whenever we gave you stewing steak, you ended up with gravy stains on your glasses."

"Oh, dear," I said, inventing the sight and immediately wishing it away. "That really does sound a bit dire."

"And I've never," said Dad, "seen anyone eat a bacon sandwich faster than you."

"Food of the gods, mate," I replied. "Maybe I should insist on being buried with a bacon sandwich cunningly concealed about my person. Well, not too cunningly. Nothing infra dig, you understand. Wouldn't want to leave the world with pig meat up my arse, now, would I? I can just see it. There he goes, the last of the Haneys, off to Avernus with a bacon sandwich, *The House at Pooh Corner,* his ATC cap badge, a packet of fags, his Stones LPs, and last but not least, a bloody great jar of Marmite."

Dad, the congenital Stoic and sapient cetacean who had never taken his offspring to task for their voluntary failure to produce children and who also (like most Anglo-Saxons) appreciated gallows humor almost as much as he relished all quips of the off-color kind, promptly emitted a buoyant croak that snailed away and then became an inauspicious wheeze.

"Avernus?" he rasped.

"Oh," I said. "The entrance to the underworld. In Italy. It's a dingy lake near Naples. 'The place where no birds fly.' If they've got any fucking sense. It's in the, ah, *Aeneid.* Which I only got to read in what they call depth thanks to you, mate—

making up the difference between what the jolly old government gave me and what it actually cost to get some Latin done
whenever I wasn't subjecting my liver to cruel and unusual
punishment."

"I suppose that's true," said Dad. "Do you think it
helped?"

"What?"

"The degree."

"Not half," I said. "Nobody gets an okay job at a decent
fucking magazine without one."

"So you like it where you are?" said Dad.

"Yes," I said. "Believe it or not, I never get bored."

"And the people you work with, you like them?"

"Yes," I said. "Even though a lot of them come from back-
grounds you and I would consider, oh, I don't know, a bit
bloody posh. But we get along fine. And in my case, of
course, the British accent helps."

"Really," said Dad, pushing his half-empty plate aside and
breaking into an ounce of Golden Virginia. "How come?"

"Well," I said, "you probably won't believe this, but an
amazing number of people on the other side of the pond seem
to think that any Brit with a vaguely—even a very vaguely—
upper-crusty accent probably comes from money and went to
Cambridge."

"Blimey," said Dad. "I had no idea."

"It's bloody well true," I said. "And it's why I end up feeling like a bumpkin in a ballroom a lot of the time."

"Well, you shouldn't."

"Well, I'm sorry, Dad. But I do. And one of these days it
might get even worse. Mind if I finish your chips?"

"All yours. And what do you mean, it might get worse?"

"You never know," I said. "I might end up somewhere more classy. Hearst, perhaps. Or the crème de la crème— Condé Nast."

"Who?" said Dad.

"I suppose you could call them the big guns," I said. "*Vogue. The New Yorker.* I'd have to be on my best behavior there."

AFTER LUNCH, Dad took an afternoon nap and I went for a walk down to Romford Town Center. I complacently surveyed, along the way, the leafless streets and dustbin-dotted avenues, the underfunded corner stores compounded of cough drops and saris, the friendless unisex hair salons, the inquisitive eyes of the graying purveyors of haddock and eels, the off-white nylon curtains moping in the single-glazed windows of ten-hutch hotels, the squirrel-faced blondes in concupiscent heels tottering arm-in-arm with Essex boys (flagrant alternations of ego and id in well-pressed slacks and blouson leather jackets), outbreaks of truancy trailing yards of possibly half-inched (meaning "pinched") football scarves, elderly women in plastic macs emerging from unkempt cafés, and, as always at that time of year, straight-backed old soldiers in flat hats and raincoats selling the stylized blood-red poppies that shriek to all Britons of this war and that war and, above all, of the lives that were lost in the First.

Once amid the ruck of stores (Virgin, Marks and Spencer, C & A), I measured time in terms of snacks and decamped three hours later, having introspectively, and happily, consumed a tea cake with coffee, a currant bun, a surreally flaccid saveloy, a sideswipe of cod roe, and, in a pub, a pale impersonation of a steak and kidney pie and a dwarfish disk of jam roly-poly stranded in a slimy bowl of superheated custard.

An hour or so thereafter, Dad donned a cap, his only cashmere scarf (a gift from Joy), his woolen gloves, and his second-best coat and, as he'd been doing five times a week for five years, slowly drove off in his final malfunctioning rust heap (a moth-eaten Fiat with two useless doors, a trunk tied closed with plastic rope, and a gaping hole in the dashboard where the radio had been) to visit his bedridden lady friend, Susan, who had multiple sclerosis and lived in a nursing home an hour's journey away.

AT HALF PAST FIVE the following morning, I peevishly clubbed the alarm clock (on loan from Dad) so hard with *The Magic Mountain* that, to my dismay and Dad's patient vexation, it broke.

Six cups of Gold Blend, a torment of bacon, two eggs, toast, a shallow bath (with outstandings of gooseflesh), and too many roll-ups and ready-mades later, Joy banged the doorbell (Pip had to work). She was just minutes ahead of Pauline and fifty-three-year-old "young Dave," into whose car I shoehorned Dad while Joy and Wendy were both chauffeured by Gillian.

"Where's Pam, John?" said Pauline. "I thought she was coming over, too."

"She'll be here tomorrow. The fun and games and constant pain of being self-employed."

"Tell me about it," said Dave.

"Did she ever meet Don?" asked Pauline.

"No," I said. "But she's heard about him, believe me. Which, I guess, makes her one of the very few Americans who know exactly where the dear old Isle of Dogs is."

We pressed on southwestward, tracking in part the easternmost extension of the Underground's District Line, through Hornchurch (once home to the wartime RAF Fighter Command base along whose disused runways and dispersals Mum had wheeled me in my pram for windblown constitutionals in 1954 and 1955), through East Ham (where Philip and Cecily Skipton had tutored the spawn of what Dad had often slyly called "the riffraff," "the rabble," "the hoi polloi," "the great unwashed," from which, he pointed out to Joy and me, "you are, of course, descended"), through Plaistow, and through Poplar (a Labour stronghold long ago, both during and before the Attlee years).

Then, having hummed south, half-circled the bend to the bottom of Westferry Road, and finally veered off to the right, we came to sad-sack rest a few doors down from a sawn-off house where towering updos, inflexible suits, and overstated lipstick were not so much in evidence as they had been and where cigarettes were, nowadays, very much poison non grata.

When the hearse arrived with Don's remains and a primary, quite magnificent black-and-yellow wreath in the unlikely (but not inappropriate) shape of a dartboard, Rose, with characteristic kindness, insisted that Joy and I sit with Dad and Ray in one of the two hired cars. Followed by a skein of mostly modest private vehicles, we drove, with infinite care and attention, a couple of hundred overcast yards (stopping in front of Don's favorite pub, where the landlord came out to pay his respects to the widow) to the grime-caked front steps of the (Anglican) Church of Christ and St. John with St. Luke's. Having helped Dad to an unstable pew in this soot-streaked, unheated Victorian dust heap, I asked him whether it was possibly the church where I had first collided with "all of us" in a festal mood as a child.

"I've no idea at all, son," said Dad. "Are you sure you're not getting it mixed up with something else?"

"I don't think so," I said.

"You're never going to believe this," fizzed Ray, who had just begun to read the order of service.

"What?" said Joy.

"They've flipping well gone and spelled his bloody name wrong," he foamed, transparently appalled by this affront to the standards of accuracy for which he had been renowned among his colleagues during his forty years with the Inland Revenue. "It's *Haney,* not *Hanney.* Who's in charge here? Jesus Christ. I think we ought to complain."

"It's a bit late now," I said. "And besides, Don would probably find it bloody hilarious."

"Maybe," said Ray. "But I shouldn't think Rosie's too pleased."

"Probably a bit pissed off," I said. "So there goes Uncle Don, my loves, not with a bang but a balls-up."

"Look sharp, you lot," said Ray as Rose's, Diane's, and Susan's sobs peaked and threatened to shove Bach aside. The piece was one Dad had played on the luckless piano that, for all I knew, still shared a kitchen-cum-boudoir with a couple of Rick's drum kits above a Chinese restaurant in Brixton. "Here comes the vicar. Blimey—it's a lady."

"So it is," I said. And thought to myself: she's cute. Her theology wasn't, though, featuring as it did a professional unwillingness (about which she was disturbingly forthcoming) to second-guess the nature of the afterlife.

By the end of the service, my shirtfront, tie, and jacket lapels had absorbed the first drops of a flash flood of tears that then made short work of three brand-new handkerchiefs and a sizable wad of tissues dispensed by a whimpering Joy with dispassionate subvention from Dad. Afterward, Don was conveyed to the City of London Cemetery (in a part of the far eastern suburbs known as Manor Park), where Nana Haney, Grandma Bush, and Grandpa had also been cremated.

Here, we endured a service less protracted and a good deal more orthodox than the doctrinal debacle that had christened the afternoon; we watched, saying nothing, as a devastated Rose shuffled back and forth, in winding sheets of rain, to read every last card stapled to the carapace of every last waterborne scrunch of half-frozen laudatory flowers; and we boarded our cars to trickle back to a house that was now half empty.

ONCE ARRIVED and having settled Dad, who was speechless from exhaustion, in a chair next to Ray, I went outside for a quick cigarette and then undertook a reconnaissance in depth of the kitchen table, which, to my amazement, was groaning with six different kinds of quiche and not much else. (Don, I learned from Rose a moment later, had grown to like it.) Gone for good, four decades deceased, leaving no trace, it suddenly seemed, but wistful thinking, half-truths, and errata, were yesterday's mollusks and beer. I found this depressing. Joy, on the other hand, was (initially) delighted. It quickly became clear, however, that the kind of quiche allowed on the Isle of Dogs did not resemble its buttercup-complexioned, better-bred cousins from Hampstead.

"Diane," said Joy, "are any of these meatless?" (Joy had by now discerned that two of the pies on offer were manifestly sausage-swamped.)

"Oh, dear," said Diane. "We've forgotten you again, haven't we? Let's have a look. This one. This one looks like cheese only. But you'll have to pick the bacon bits off the top."

"Oh," said Joy. "Maybe I'll just have a cup of tea, in that case."

"Milk and sugar?"

"Er, no thanks."

"What? Nothing?"

"A slice of lemon would be nice," said Joy.

"You what?" said Diane, her kindly face clouded by the same mixture of disbelief and disgust that I exhibit when exposed to a dessert containing kumquats. "Lemon? I'm afraid we don't have any. Sorry."

"Bad luck, Joy," I said. "You're being a nuisance again. Tea with nothing it is, then. I'll have one too, Diane."

"I don't know how you can drink it like that," said Diane.

"It's not by choice in my case," I said. "I'm slightly allergic to milk and, so my doctor says, a bit banged up in the blood-sugar department."

"Blimey," said Diane, "I'm surprised you're still walking. I hope you're not allergic to beer."

"Well, I wasn't the last time I looked. But I prefer wine

these days. It's rumored to be a more civilized way to get
pissed."

"Dad didn't go much on wine."

"I find that very easy to believe."

"But I quite like it. Not the really cheap stuff, though."

"I should bloody well hope not."

"Here, your dad looks like he needs a cup of tea. Milk and
two sugars for him, I suppose?"

"Of course," said Joy. "Some things never change."

"They certainly don't," I said. "Thank God. Would you
give the old boy his cuppa, Diane? I need a carbon monoxide
break. And maybe a bit of a walk."

The southern route from No. 43 Harbinger Road to that
part of the Isle of Dogs known as Island Gardens brought me,
in a matter of unbelievably bone-chilling minutes, to the
northern bank of the Thames, which I'd first seen in 1960.
We'd boarded a steamer near Blackfriars Bridge for an outing
to Kew. My mother said many years later that I had, to her
surprise—this I remembered—fled the flock of punters at the
sharp end of the scow for the solitude of standing (both paws
affixed to a burly banana sandwich) at the vessel's empty rear,
silently snatching the unlooked-for prize of an uninterrupted
sight of a million landmarks. She'd followed me, and, so she
said, I'd eventually asked—but this I've forgotten—if we
were anywhere near where Rose and Don lived. "Not really,
dear," she'd said. "You like them, don't you?"

I did indeed, I thought now, while lighting another Camel
and shedding a freeze-dried tear or two. And I still do. And I
always will. Because what I experienced in their house was
undiluted happiness.

I took a last look at the darkening water and trudged back up Harbinger Road for two more cups of desolate tea, no quiche, and half a biscuit.

FIVE DAYS LATER, Pam and I took a taxi to Heathrow at six in the morning. Dad, who had risen at four to begin making breakfast for us—sloppy scrambled eggs, desiccated bacon, barely browned toast, butter-flecked honey and marmalade (for Pam), equally vandalized Marmite (for me)—flapped farewell (a skinny flamingo in underfed dressing gown, emaciated slippers, and tenuous vest) from his kitchen window.

Shortly after takeoff, Pam inquired: "You lot take it seriously, don't you? Romford Town Center. Yesterday afternoon. I couldn't believe it. Everybody had a poppy on. Not just the old folks. Teenagers. Kids. Babies. Everyone."

"Yes," I said, "we do. Extremely fucking seriously. That was the worst fucking war ever fought, if you don't count the Russian front—in World War II. Three quarters of a million of our lot killed. Another quarter million from the Empire. God knows how many more wounded. And God alone knows how many others sent . . . well, not completely barking mad. But not exactly what you'd call—well-balanced. Possibly including my grandpa. He wasn't the happiest camper in the world. Having to use the bayonet probably isn't all that good for a young man's mental health."

"Makes sense."

"You know, he used to get these really black moods. Every now and then. Smiling—or, at least, quite contented—one minute, and then clamming up. Completely fucking stone-faced for hours."

"Shit," said Pam. "I have wondered, from what you've told me—maybe he was fucked up."

"And who could blame him?" I sighed. "Wasn't exactly fabulous news for his daughters, of course. He was insanely strict with them. And sometimes, according to Mum, who only began to tell Joy about it a couple of years ago, a bit bloody brutal."

"Oh," said Pam. "Why didn't you tell me about that?"

"Figured you already knew enough about what makes *me* tick. The poorhouse back then. And the poorhouse now. Meaning Mum. And having no idea of where I belong—the nicely dressed kid whose Dad drove, and still drives, a wreck. And I know it makes me difficult to live with sometimes. What with your being such an incurable optimist—I'm sorry."

"You should have told me that Grandpa stuff. It's like all the other stuff. It explains things."

"I'm sorry, honey, but there are definitely times when being explained *really* gets me down."

"Well, as far as I'm concerned, John, it helps."

"I wouldn't say that. Not always."

BY THE TIME we reached cruising altitude, Pam was engrossed in a book on the Wiener Werkstätte and I had just learned from Jack London's *The People of the Abyss* that on the day of King Edward VII's coronation, the "East End, as a whole, remained in the East End and got drunk." Outside, the sun, in a fury, had spawned an empyrean of diabetic bluebells and refrigerated steel. Inside, the vapors of breakfast began to career.

"You hungry?" said Pam. "I think I am."

"You won't be when it gets here," I griped, suddenly feeling, for no reason I could fathom, as if all the bad blood from a rotten filet had been hosed into my mouth.

The airplane began to outpace Scotland. The sun shone harder. The bluebells drooped. All the sharpened spades that ever were began to sparkle. Half an hour later, Pam said: "It's always so good to see your dad. He asked me not to leave it another five years before I come over again. So I won't. I promise."

"Actually, hon," I replied. "I'm not sure we can leave it another year. He's in terrible shape."

"I could see that," said Pam. "I'm not blind."

"I know that. But. Ugh. This is worse than terrible. He's on the way out, and he knows it. Deep down. Way down. For certain."

"Oh?"

"He took me into his bedroom just before we left. Showed me where his papers were. Life insurance. The grown-up stuff. It's serious."

"Oh."

"We have to go back *early* next year, hon. Soon. Sometime this spring. April. May. June at the absolute latest."

"June," said Pam. "End of June. I should be done with my New York Gift Show orders by then."

"Fine," I said. "I'll tell him right away. It'll give him something to fucking well look forward to."

Which he did, until May 23 of the following year, when his airways suddenly found themselves completely obstructed forever.

CHAPTER 12

A Nonconsolatory Splurge of Meursault

. . . .

THE FIRST INNUENDO OF DAD'S SUFFOCATION, LAST GASP, AND release from the confines of mortality came in the guise of a message from Jackie, left on my answering machine at four o'clock in the morning on a Sunday. Accustomed as I was, however, to my aunt's increasing propensity to ignore the fact that the East Coast and Redbridge are five hours apart, I failed to push playback till one in the afternoon.

Once I had gagged on the news, relayed to my auntie by Reg, that Dad's minaciously short-winded frame had just been rushed to Oldchurch Hospital, the rack-rent lazaretto where I had reflexively frowned when a scalpel's intrusion spelled spasms of flashlight and seizures of bawling where once in umbilical darkness I'd dozed to the clockwork berceuse of Mum's heart, I called Jackie back.

Dad, she said, had "gone" (apparently alone and unattended) an hour earlier. Joy and Pip had arrived about twenty minutes later, having been reached by the sister in charge of

the ward ("Can you come now, my dear? I really think you
have to") upon their return from a motorbike outing to Kew.
They found the gurney on which he'd been deposited
posthumously and parked (intelligent head drawn elastically
back, astounded mouth agape) in a utility room near the mor-
tuary, meanly hemmed in by limp crenellations of discount
detergent and teetering bastions of harsh disinfectants like
Brobat, Domestos, and Vim.

"The worst thing," said Joy, when I called her, "was,
when we got there, nobody knew where he was. Or how he
was. They'd actually managed to lose him."

"Did anyone say they were fucking well sorry?"

"Barely."

"Idiots."

"But it didn't really matter by then. I was already in shock.
I sort of knew—when we got into the car that we were going
to be too late. Pip drove like a maniac, and I sat there thinking, It probably isn't worth it."

"I think I'd have felt the same way," I said, picturing Dad
as a fish denied water and Pip wildly giving his weather-
veined Volvo the Michael Schumacher treatment.

"Mind you," I added, "knowing Dad, he might just have
found it amusing."

"Maybe," said Joy. "Maybe not. But the first thing I
thought was, Sidelined again. And I said to the nurse—the
one who finally found him—'Why is he in here? Why didn't
anyone know where he was? This is my lovely father.' "

PAM AND I crossed the Atlantic a week, further tears, and an
autopsy later, by which time Dad's clay—neck adjusted,

mouth closed, hair combed, and fingers, if need be, I pondered, unclenched—had been consigned to the no-frills care of Cooperative Funeral Services. Pam, determined to wangle an upgrade to a better class of seating by virtue of being bereft, spun the British Airways clerk a melancholy story of the sob-conductive kind—to no effect, we self-pityingly thought, until we were briskly summoned forward to a much nicer part of the plane not too long before the aircraft's measured rumble grew into an unrestrained roar.

A half hour later, three parts of a four-part breakfast politely emerged as melon (confused), Ryvita (connected), and a twist of cured fish (without flavor). I focused for a moment, as my fleeting appetite fled, on the eggs, as runaway, runamok, formlessly scrambled as those Dad had so stubbornly concocted on a dark Sunday morning six months earlier.

As Halifax fell victim to rearview and the imminence of Gander, I took a first scattershot stab at a eulogy, failed in the course of the five hours that followed to scribble so much as a sentence even remotely worthy of its subject, and finally, as Belfast (pronounced by the captain) slipped beneath the starboard wing, solicited a third (and last before landfall) gin with a drip feed of tonic. I then returned to a Penguin selection of Swinburne, and, between stanzas, witlessly recalled the tirade that Joy had unleashed (her customary composure resonantly repressed by a deadweight of rank indignation) at an administrator at the hospital where Dad had been mislaid: "I'm sorry . . ." she'd sniffed, then briefly subsided, slowly about-faced, succumbed to sheer fury, and snapped: "But this just isn't good enough. It's just not good enough. It just isn't fair. It. Just. Is. Not. Fair."

"So, Joy," I said the following morning while wrapped in

a Saks Fifth Avenue dressing gown, trying not to choke on a duty-free Camel, and blearily peering by quasi-Catholic candlelight at a tiny photo propped against an eggcup on Joy's mantel and showing Denis, in a sleeve-free V-neck, with his newly christened daughter (looking like an inverted tub of yogurt) in his arms. "Dad's send-off. Nondenominational. Yes? You said we had a choice."

"Of course," said Joy. "For the most part. Just a couple of hymns he liked. The ones you suggested. 'All People That on Earth Do Dwell.' And the Bunyan thing. 'To Be a Pilgrim.' Right?"

"Right," I said, coughing, depleted, back in the pews at St. Mary's and virtually yelling my favorite hymn. "The good tunes. But no 'forgive us our trespasses.' Dad didn't go much on that kind of thing. Can't think why—living a dog's life might have had something to do with it. You got that past them okay?"

"More or less. The lady vicar they're giving us seemed a bit surprised. 'But if you're going to have the hymns, dear, why don't you want the Lord's Prayer?' I felt a bit sorry for her."

"Well, she'll just have to deal with it, won't she?" I said, wondering why on earth any self-respecting cleric would balk at an inconvenient example of the infinite variability of human preference. "I'm sure she'll cope. We won't be the only cortège of hymn-singing skeptics ever to have hurtled through the not-so-pearly gates of the South Essex Crematorium. By the way, where is that?"

"Upminster."

"Perfect. Yet another byword for boredom. Just like

Ongar and Romford. Live uneventfully, die uneventfully. Why the hell not."

"And instead of the commendation—" said Joy.

"You got that past her as well?" I interposed.

"—I'll be reading something I found in *Middlemarch*. I've adapted it. A bit."

"Hmmm," I said. "Did you know she did the first English translation of David Friedrich Strauss's *Life of Jesus*?"

"Who?" said Joy.

"George Eliot."

"No," said Joy, "I didn't. Does it matter?"

"No," I replied. "I was just curious."

"Well, don't be," she said. "We're running out of time, John. It's Tuesday and the funeral's on Thursday. And tomorrow we're going to Romford."

"We are?" I said. "Why?"

"To sort through his things. For a start."

"Shit," I said. "I'm not too sure I can face that. Can't Reg do it?"

"For God's sake," said Joy. "It's our job, not Reg's. And I don't fancy it either but I'm going to do it anyway, and you're going to help me. And we've got to work out what to keep. Bits and bobs. Books. Photos. Records. And give Reg a hand with the housecleaning. I'm sure he's doing his best, but it's not what I'd call his strong point. Then we come back here and do the food. And the book of remembrance. And Pip's going off to IKEA to buy some wineglasses. Which gives us, you and me, a couple of days to get these speeches written. How's yours coming along?"

"It's not," I sniveled. "I can't bloody think straight on

planes. And last week was hell at the office." (I was now working as copy chief at *Men's Journal*.) "How are you doing with yours?"

"Not much better," she sniffed. "I've been crying a lot."

"So how do we do this?"

"I don't know," said Joy. "Get cleaned up. Go for a walk. Clear our heads. Have an early lunch. And get on with it. Up in my studio's probably best. We each get a desk. And the light's good."

"Fine," I said. "But I'm going to need some booze. Oh— what about the music? Everything squared away there?"

"Yes," said Joy. " 'Jesu, Joy of Man's Desiring.' On the organ. On the way in. And Beethoven's Sixth. Pip bought the CD. At the end. The final movement. The shepherds' song. He adored it."

A few minutes later, Mum called to apologize for having taken "such a long time" to make up her mind and announced she thought it might be best if she didn't attend the funeral.

HAVING DULY SLOGGED in a shrinking daze (and a hasty glaze of heedless cigarette smoke) twice around the near deserted grounds of a neighborhood museum founded by a family of tannin tycoons with a fetish for stuffed animals, Joy and I returned home. We shattered a salad, emptied the neck of a green-cheeked bottle of savagely chilled Sancerre, and went upstairs.

"I honestly don't know where to begin," I said. "How do I do Dad justice in five bloody minutes?"

"Er—by sticking to the point," replied Joy. "Dispensing with the peripherals and the tangents."

"I see," I said. "Okay. So—I do have a handful of adjectives."

"Well," said Joy, "that's better than nothing. Go on."

"Kind," I gurgled. "Gentle. Patient. Remarkably patient. And a right fucking miracle that was. Imagine having to put up with you, me, and Mum in the same bloody house and back garden for more than twenty years. I'd have hopped it after the first ten minutes. This wine's very good. Where'd you get it?"

"Harvey Nicks. Pip knows one of the buyers."

"What else? Tolerant. Self-sacrificing. Not remotely racist. Very unusual for a working-class bloke of his generation. Good provider, despite the fact that money was always a struggle. Bloody good father, even though he never knew his own dad. Very down-to-earth, unlike his airy-fairy son. Practical—ditto. Cheerful—which I'll never get the hang of. Not remotely bitter about his lack of advantages. That's important. That's really important. And then there's the fact that he didn't have the usual working-class chip on his shoulder. So what do you think? Of that lot?"

"Not bad," she replied.

"And you?"

"Something a bit different. I thought I'd start with the fact that Dad was, well, a motherly father."

"I see. The girl's perspective."

"Well, it's true. Look at how he used to bathe us. And read to us at bedtime. And cook. And sew. Remember? He made that dress I wore in a Christmas play at primary school. Out of a sheet and some ribbons."

"Nothing if not versatile," I said. "Quite the good all-rounder."

"And he never shouted. He never—ever—hit us. And he made me feel safe as well. Remember the sound of his key in the door? When he came home from a late shift?"

"Hmmm," I said, remembering lying awake for hours until the very same moment. "Now that you mention it, that little click had the same effect on me."

I paused.

"You know, it's funny you said that. Because, oh—no, it's ridiculous. I feel . . . well, kind of abandoned. Completely alone. And I know I've got Pam. And that's fine, much more than just fine. (Though I really don't know how the hell she puts up with me.) And Mum's still around. But . . . the way I feel now. It's so completely unfamiliar. I can hardly describe it. It's this emptiness that feels like it's going to go on. Forever. No relief in sight. No cure. Just on and on. Forever. I'm sorry. You were saying?"

"Where was I? Oh. Yes. Even when he was angry with us, it was really cut and dried. He was . . . sort of restrained. And nothing ever threw him. Nothing. And if it did, he never let us know it."

"That's true," I said. "He just bloody well got on with stuff. In difficult situations. Of which, I think it's fair to say, he had to deal with far too fucking many. Remember that day in Wellbourne? In Sussex. He took us out in a rowing boat. Just you and me, Mum wasn't feeling so hot."

"Oh, yes," said Joy. "Wellbourne. Sort of a holiday camp, wasn't it? We stayed in an upturned lifeboat."

"Yes, we did. Very quaint. But not particularly cozy."

"The place with the donkeys. Run by that beefy ex-commando bloke who was always running around in shorts. Offering people shooting lessons. And his peculiar wife.

Nigel and Nancy Something. Yes? She had a thing about sundials, remember? Couldn't get enough of them. I was very disappointed there at first."

"Why?" I said. "Nigel and Nancy Norman-Walker were very nice to us. Very nice. Even though they were, let's face it, more than a little bit upper."

"Not because of them," said Joy. "Because there wasn't a beach."

"No," I said, "there wasn't. Just. Well. Miles and miles of, I don't know, mud flats? I suppose you could call them that. Remember when the tide went out? All those channels appeared. And the water was so unbelievably clear. And the birds. God. The birds. Millions more than at Bournemouth. Up in the trees. And down by the water. And out on the marsh. Wading birds. All kinds. It was all you could hear. The wind. The birds. The donkeys every now and then. And it all died down in the afternoons. I couldn't believe how quiet it was. Which is strange. I mean, Ongar was as dead as a doornail all the time. Maybe it's the silences near the sea that are different. We shut out the ones we're used to."

"I do remember that," said Joy. "Especially the donkeys. Larry. The grumpy one. And Lucy. She was sweet. It was nice, in the end. In a weird kind of way. We were quite small then, weren't we?"

"Not so very small," I said, ripping open more wine and, without noticing, slitting an index finger on the foil. "It was after our last trip to Bournemouth. So Dad took us out in that boat, and the sea disappeared. And he got us back a fair bit of the way by rowing along one of those channels. And there was poor old Mum in a panic, as always, waving from some kind of floodgate. And Dad said: 'I'll have to abandon ship,

I'm afraid. You two stay *right* where you are.' And he dragged the boat across the sludge. And I still can't quite believe it. Which was when I saw this crab right next to Dad. Must have been at least an inch wide. I'd never seen a real one before. And I started screaming. And that set you off. And Dad just kept pulling. Up to his knees in bloody mud, sweating like a pig with his glasses half off. In his nylon shirt and theater-going trousers, out in the middle of nowhere, pulling a bloody boat across a quarter of a mile of mud. With you and me in it. Just pulling. And pulling. And pulling."

Joy began to cry and said: "You've cut yourself, John. Can't you feel it?"

DESPITE THE CONTINUED existence of Reg, whose well-meant exertions with tin-whistle dustpan, troglodyte mop, and grit-nippled bubo of dusters had, to Joy's amazement, swept every inch of the sitting room, kitchen, and hallway unbearably clean, Dad's flat felt endlessly deserted the following morning. Bitterly nursing the nub of a breath mint and a mouthful of strangely weak tea, I scowled at the loss of the landfill and internally sneered at its barren replacement by a newly laundered tablecloth.

A few minutes later, leaving Pam and Pip to sift through a shoe box and two battered albums in search of some snaps that might be worth including in the book of remembrance, Joy (sternly) and I (with no esprit de corps at all) set foot in Dad's sanctum, slowly swung open the doors of his closet, and regretfully siphoned a feeble cascade of unprepossessing clothes into a bumble of trash bags.

"Oh, fuck," I said. "This feels like bloody stealing. Feels

like he's alive. And kicking. And might walk in and stop us."

"That'd be nice," said Joy. "Very nice. Any of these suits of any interest?"

"No," I said, paying little attention. "The one I bloody well did want seems to have disappeared."

"Oh?" said Joy. "Which one's that?"

"The two-piece he wore to your wedding," I rejoined. "The silver-gray thing. He told me it cost him a fortune."

"That was a nice suit."

"So where the hell is it?" I puzzled. "He can't have thrown the bloody thing away."

"Maybe he did."

"Dad? Throw decent clothes away? I don't think so."

"Who knows? If I'd been him, I don't think I'd have kept it. That was a rotten bloody day."

"Did me in."

"What about this cardigan?"

"Hmmm—the classic old bloke's sensible zip-up. No."

"You'll be an old bloke one of these days. And feeling the cold the way Dad did. You should keep it."

"If you insist," I said sullenly, feeling slightly sick, shivering at the thought of myself twenty or thirty years hence—maybe more stooped and, perish the thought, woolens-fixated than Dad.

"I feel so empty," said Joy. "So empty. No nice kind daddy. Not anymore. All over. All gone. Forever."

AFTER A DINNER of bell peppers (red, yellow, green), five kinds of goat cheese, convulsions of spelt, and a fanfare of organic soy, Joy and Pam and I spent the evening (Sancerre-soaked on my part) gazing at photos snatched from the sinking of Denis's coracle vitae. We sat amid rakish candle flames and the reek of espresso; cigarettes plumed on all sides, wine bottles stood guard over leavings.

"Are you sure he's in this one?" The shot showed a dozen young men of twelve or thirteen in what we assumed to be Alexandra Orphanage blazers and ties.

"No," said Joy. "But Dick or Dave might be. And, well, it's the orphanage. It's got to be. It's important. What about this one?"

"Oh, yes. Private Haney wearing a fez. In Cairo. In 1943. Says so on the back. That's in."

"I like that one," said Pam. "It captures his smile. And that was why I picked it."

"I think that might have been the only fucking smile he managed there. He couldn't stand the place."

"And here he is with a bunch of his mates in Gibraltar," said Joy. "Up on the fortress. Everyone merrily puffing away and smiling—they look like they're on holiday."

"They were," I said. "That was 1946. Dad spent a year there. Two hours' typing a day with no bloody war to worry about. He was in the garrison rowing team, you know."

"Really?" said Joy.

"Oh, yes," I said. "And a very good team it was, apparently. Raced the Navy in Gibraltar harbor. And guess who fucking won. The Army. Much to the Navy's annoyance."

"Do you think this one's too bizarre?" said Joy.

"Possibly," I said, squinching at a four-by-six of a fox-faced Dad looking almost louche in a suit unescorted by shirt, vest, or tie. "Out in the country and—I'm guessing—being a bit of lad."

"Bit of a lad, eh?" said Pam. "Not quite sure I can see that. Not that he was all that buttoned-down."

"Oh, I think he had it in him," I replied. "He was a bloody Cockney. And bloody good at dancing. Which isn't the *most* asexual activity in the world. Actually, I remember Ray saying Eileen once said: 'You're a very good dancer, Ray. But nobody dances like Denis.' Really. I'm not kidding."

"This one?" asked Joy, proffering an image of a seventh-decade Dad, in jeans and a windcheater, looking a great deal less than absorbed in Allen Carr's *The Easy Way to Stop Smoking* while sitting in the garden at the commune and being kept company by his black-clad, orange-haired daughter.

"Definitely," I said, torching another Camel.

"I liked the commune," said Pam. "The location, I mean. It was peaceful. Didn't quite get the politics, though."

"You weren't the only one," I said. "Talk about making Lenin look broad-minded."

"Oh, it wasn't like that," said Joy, handing me a shot of Mum and Dad ensconced on a tandem. "What about this one?"

"Love the matching shorts and shirts," I said. "Probably out with their cycling club. Rainham to Southend and back in a day. Bit bloody tough on the hemorrhoids, though. Or maybe that's how Dad got them."

"Bournemouth," said Joy, studying a picture of a lollipop-wielding three-year-old hand in hand with Dad at water's edge and looking blissfully misshapen in her piss-proof polythene pants and frilly-brimmed lily-white sun hat. "That's important."

Mum and Dad, 1951

"Dad looks pretty tough in that one," said Pam.

"Oh yes," I said. "The whipcord effect. Skinny but muscular with it. He apparently thought nothing of marching all day with a Bren gun stashed on his shoulder. I got to take one apart once. They're actually bloody heavy."

"Was that in the ATC?" asked Pam.

"Yes, dear, where else? Light machine guns weren't allowed at youth clubs."

"This one?" said Pip.

"Good choice. Having a hectic day out with the Multiple Sclerosis Society. How is Susan, by the way?"

"Not too awful," said Joy. "According to her niece. But

terribly upset about Dad. And this one? On the Circle Line boat. With the Statue of Liberty looming in the background. He looks so happy."

"He was," I said. "Must have been that plastic cup of jug stuff I bought him. I'm kidding."

"He really enjoyed that trip," said Pam. "I think we showed him a great time."

"You did," said Joy. "He talked about it for months. Months and months and months. He really liked that 'slap-up feed'— that's what he called it—you gave him in Pennsylvania."

"Slap-up feed," I murmured to no one. "Probably a term you only use if you've grown up uncommonly hungry."

"This one's a must," said Joy. "In the back garden at Mornington Road. Making eggs and bacon. For Angelika and those friends of hers from Rotterdam. A month before he died. Angie says the effort nearly killed him. She offered to help, but he just wouldn't let her. Typical. And there's this one. From the week before he died."

"Who took it?" I asked, taking in a beaming Dad, with cigarette, at the front door of 52A.

"One of his friends from the Commercial. A few of them popped over for a pub lunch and a bit of a reminisce."

At this point, my own reminiscing propelled me to the guest lavatory, where I curled up on the floor and silently cried, undisturbed, for an hour while Joy and Pam made potato salad (from Pam's recipe) and Pip washed and dried all the glasses.

AT TEN THE NEXT MORNING, attired as if fused for an evening of cocktails and self-adoration in SoHo, we stopped at the funeral home for a last look at Dad and found him sporting a suit that I was convinced he would never have been seen dead in, a wrinkled coalition two bulimic shades of ill-considered blue and dejected, at the sternum, by a clumsily knotted knit tie.

"This," I said, looking askance at Joy and suddenly feeling angry and humiliated on Dad's behalf, "is from a charity shop. It has to be. I know he had a few cheap suits, but nothing quite this nasty."

"This is one of Dad's suits," said Joy, no longer a pudding-faced infant but a serious-looking woman in her forties with not-quite-hollow cheeks, a torrent of sandy hair, and an astronomical dental bill that had been the salvation of her two most imperative incisors. "They were all like this. Didn't you notice? But he's shrunk. So it looks like somebody else's."

"Oh, well." My inferiority complex made a comeback I hadn't been expecting. "There's nothing we can do about it now."

"And his nose isn't shaved," said Joy, her eyes welling. "It looks like a cactus."

"Wouldn't disagree with that," I sighed. "Once again—you get what you pay for. Particularly when your life insurance isn't up to snuff."

"Are you okay, Pam?" said Joy.

Pam was crying.

"Not really," Pam said. "Dad was one of the kindest men I ever knew. And there aren't many kind men around."

The room now seemed even quieter than I could ever have imagined death to be.

———

AT MORNINGTON ROAD, a forest of flowers had sprung up in the parking space forsaken by the Fiat and was now being soberly and sociably surrounded by a minor herd of largely bespectacled late-middle-aged and elderly men and a sprinkling of smartly dressed (and, it seemed, much less myopic) women. Pauline (minus "young Dave," who was laid up at home with his knees out of sorts owing to inordinate boiler repair), an unaccompanied cousin Diane (no longer the excited nineteen-year-old looking forward to a honeymoon in Dubrovnik but a smartly attired woman in her thirties who worked in real estate and had two children), and an elfin fifty-something named Joanna, a cha-cha fiend who had once, it was rumored (and Joy and I hoped), taken considerably more than a shine to a subsequently red-faced Dad at a New Year's Eve party in The Hague. (Aunt Rose and Susan were away on vacation, with Susan's two daughters in tow, at a holiday camp in Kent.)

When the Cooperative cars arrived (overseen by a kindly Scot in his sixties and otherwise staffed by four young men with haircuts straight out of reform school), Pam, Pip, and Joy and I squeezed into one as lead mourners with Ray (graying, leukemic, and sparing, today, with the jokes) and Jackie (seventy-five, hard of hearing, dressed to the nines of days gone by in polyester) and drifted (as if in a dream on my part) through moderate traffic to the place of public burning. There, we took our seats in a tinpot chapel and gloomily gazed as—to the highly irksome sound of "Jesu, Joy of Man's Desiring" being butchered by someone with no sense of phrasing—the delinquents transferred Dad's coffin to a catafalque of sorts haphazardly fringed with a crust of pleated curtains the color of devil's-food cake.

Two hymns and two speeches (mine overshadowed, and justly, by Joy's) in a mere twenty minutes (two thirds of the time the contract allowed) gave way to exit of bone bin, stumble of drapes, Beethoven's vision of "Happy and thankful feelings after the storm," a conversation-free return to Romford, and an almost heated altercation with the self-effacing Scotsman concerning the size of his tip.

"Thanks, mate," I said, handing him seventy pounds. "You guys did great. That's thirty for you. And a tenner each for the lads."

"No, no, no," he croaked, pushing the money back at me. "That's far too much, mate. You can't do that. It's far too much. Really. A fiver each is fine. Come on, now. Twenty-five quid and we'll call it quits. Not a penny more."

His minions seemed dumbstruck.

"Look," I said, "take it. This is how we do things in New York."

I SPENT THAT EVENING wantonly engrossed in a rustic but not undrinkable white from northern Sardinia. The next day, I forswore the alcohol, if only in the short term, in favor of a walk in Crystal Palace Park, a constitutional of which, thanks to the wine, I was in considerable need.

It's a strange place, Crystal Palace Park, amassing as it does odds, sods, clumps, and clods of the landscape and stonework relating to the outsize house of glass that sustained the Great Exhibition of 1851 and burned down in 1936. On its

fringe stands the fabled (in England, at any rate) Crystal
Palace television transmitter mast, a structure I like to think
quickened the pulse of every communications engineer of
Dad's generation. Also within its environs is a lake whose
banks are littered with statues representing early Victorian
paleontology's best stab at the likely appearance of a number
of prehistoric reptiles.

Toward the end of my hungover circumscription of this
improbable amenity, which blends so very queerly apparitions both ancient and modern, I came across a brightly
painted cesspit of a van that stank of cheap meat and displayed a blackboard headed by the two words that, especially
when quickly conjoined by an imprecise and unhygienic
scribble, still mean more to me than most others in the dialects
found to the south of the Antonine Wall: BACON and SAND-
WICHES. In response to my order, the potbellied owner pulled
several pink ratlines of scrap end of pork from a stained-steel
trough mantled with nine feet of polythene as muck-maned as
Crackerjack's fly-wear.

Unfurling as tooth-caked, as V-shaped, as gum-ruffed, as
drool-drenched, subconscious, and brutish a grin as that of an
appetitive tyrannosaur systemically aroused by the sight of an
expiring pterodactyl, I looked on in beatitudes as the grill
snickered, spat, simmered, sneezed, wheezed, and popped and
then, by way of gauche summation, stuck out tongues of seb-
orrheic smoke. A moment or two later—eternity seeming—
I was handed a welcoming, wide-agape wad of spongiform
starch feverishly gagging on a steam-sheathed heap of
serenely dispirited porker.

To sever the rind as surgically as possible and prevent it
from stretching and snapping and scattering spittle and spots

of grease several feet in all directions, I bit down demonically hard. At the same moment, a peremptory Concorde screeked and needled, surged and slammed, its cuneiform way over-head, shattering my concentration. I felt as nonplussed as a vapid Neanderthal abruptly surprised by an unapologetically malevolent intruder.

Another sandwich, then another and another as parents and children departed in untidy droves. England, I now knew, would always be home but also impossibly distant, a place I could never recover completely even if some future combina-

*Joy scatters Dad's ashes into the
Thames near Kew, November 1999*

tion of time, caprice, upset, sheer disillusionment, compulsion, and contrary luck were to force me to go back for good.

Next came more grief, a renewal of greed, a nagging need for waterspouts of wine. It was time to go home to diced zucchini, to a nonconsolatory splurge of Meursault, to the figments of war and the fractures of peace, to one more day of our silences speaking unreadable volumes. Time to renew an unwanted acquaintance with torments unvoiced, with unaccustomed agonies as immovably self-immured as the light from the candles, which, perpetually replenished, burned three muffled floors beneath the suitcase, stacked in Joy's attic, that now contained all that was left of our father apart from his ashes.

Certificates of birth and death, a medal he hadn't thought much of (the Italy Star), his aging (and unusable) Instamatic, a reel of much-faded Super-8 film, a hacksaw, a miniature Casio keyboard, a mushroom-shaped Bakelite tool designed to assist in the echt-frugal darning of socks, and two monophonic LPs that long disregard, undue warmth, and the poorly monitored overuse of artificial diamonds had eventually rendered worthless. Copland's *Rodeo*, Beethoven's Fifth, and segmented highlights from *Hoffmann* were, it seemed, like their owner, no longer with us. Only *Seven Brides for Seven Brothers* and *Schwanengesang* had survived.

The park, no matter where I looked, seemed empty.

CHAPTER 13

Drip-dry Shirts, Spilt Milk,
and Sugared Almonds

. . . .

I RETURNED TO LONDON FOR A STRICTLY (OR SO I HOPED)
nonfunereal visit with Joy at the end of August 2001. By then,
I was working as copy chief at *Gourmet* and Pam, understand-
ably exhausted by my continuing unwillingness to deal with
depression and a drinking problem, both of which had grown
much worse following Dad's demise, had asked for a trial
separation. Upon my arrival, early on a Monday afternoon,
Joy, guessing correctly that green tea and tempeh would not
be at the top of my wish list for the next few days, took me out
to lunch at a new (and reputedly presentable) neighborhood
greasy spoon.

The enterprise turned out to be so new that the cooking
was taking place amid the detritus of breakneck construction.
Undeterred by jet lag, however, or by the jury-rigged look of
the joint, I scrutinized the blackboard with a good deal more
concentration than I had managed to bring to bear on David

Malouf's *An Imaginary Life* during a flight spent in naked fear of distant storms and lightning. Reaching a decision, I quickly ordered two fried eggs, chips, bacon, beans, tomatoes, sausages, fried bread, and (no mewling milk, no *sucre*) a notably un-English reorganization of tea. This was a gluttonous amassment of food for a single person. The proprietress, though, barely squirmed. Joy made do with a mumbled imposition for instantaneous coffee with milk and a fried-egg sandwich.

The weather being warm, she then gave vent to a zest for sequestration in the café's impoverished excuse for a garden, which revealed itself as a half-baked *hortus conclusus* that would not have appealed to Augustine. We were now quite alone in a squalor of concrete with a causeway of paint cans in one slipshod corner, a tumble of heartbroken weeds in another, and, in the middle, an alienated table inoperably pierced by an irate umbrella on one-man parade at an angle. The food, however, in mammoth reproach to its fallen milieu, proved divine: impertinent eggs, refractory chips, a wrangle of bacon, a tangle of beans, a revenge of tomatoes (a study in scarlet), a reprobate contraire of self-serving sausages (a scintillating shade of *brun* and spangled with a splat or two of all-devouring mustard), a black-lipped bonanza of bickering mushrooms, and three buttered gun decks of toast.

"That wasn't too bad," I said, having punctured and crushed one last bean. "Fair to middling—as the education I had says of rejects. I'd come here again. Which is exactly what I said after my first nervous trip to a pretty expensive French place. Doing some 'restaurant research' for the magazine. With a friend who works at Hearst."

"Oh," said Joy, the chlorophyll-chloroformed capable

cook who can never get enough of Manhattan. "Where was that?"

"La Capeline," I said. "Particularly decadent chocolate soufflé."

"That sounds good," she lusted.

"And," I continued, "foie gras so depraved it's to die for. Followed by the most debased duck à l'orange I guess I've ever had."

"Less appealing—but nice for you, I'm sure."

"It was," I said, remembering how hard-pressed I'd been to focus on my food and pretend to ignore my dining companion's super-short jet-black cocktail dress and hyper-magnetic fishnets. "And is, if you happen to like that kind of thing. Which, and you probably won't believe this, I'm sometimes not *entirely* sure I do. It's odd. I can normally eat that kind of crap—as opposed to this crap—without so much as blinking. But every now and then, I suddenly find myself wondering, What am I doing here? Where in heaven's name are the equality police? Why the *fuck* is this being allowed?"

"Hmmm," said Joy, with a patient smile. "I wouldn't tie yourself in too many knots over that one."

"I won't," I said, my thoughts for a moment intercut by greasepaint steam escaping a dent in a long-ago Lancashire hotpot. "But it's just so strange, the timeless appeal this garbage has for me. Even though I've been exposed to quite a bit of the good stuff. And there are times when the 'good' stuff scares me. Did I ever tell you my Gramercy Avenue Bistro story?"

"No."

"Long time ago now," I said. "Maybe '88 or '89. Very nice place. Went with a couple of friends of Pam's who had a bit of money—not much, but a lot more than she and I did. Got dolled up by our standards back then. Meaning dowdy. And the staff had all four of us sized up in seconds. But they're good, they're really good. They don't show it, but you know that they know. And, oh, I don't know—it was excellent. All of it. The food. The service. It was the best place, by far, I'd ever been to. But I couldn't help looking around. At all the blue hair. And the thousand-dollar suits. And the deference. I think it was the deference that did it. I'd never been deferred to at all before, let alone insincerely. And after dessert, with dessert wine, I went out for a cig. Across the street and a few doors down. And I thought, I can't go back in there. I don't belong there. And I brought it all up. The Dungeness crab, the grass-fed steak, the booze, the panna cotta. And you know what struck me later? Much, much later?"

"What?"

"It's actually ridiculous," I said. "Completely ridiculous. But I thought, That was my inoculation against upscale food. That something like that had to happen to enable me to get through meals like that in the future without feeling guilty. Or making a fool of myself. Having a bit of a breakdown. Or laughing out loud."

"What on earth are you talking about?" said Joy. "A breakdown? Laughing out loud? You can't be serious."

"Oh, I'm serious," I said. "It all goes back to that sense of exclusion I've gone on about before, that feeling of not belonging."

"Oh," said Joy.

"Yes," I said. "That one."

"I think you make too much of it at times," she said, almost grimly. Then she smiled, and went on: "On the other hand, though, I can't say I blame you. I dread to think how I would have been if I'd ended up somewhere like KEGS. All that regimentation."

"Regimentation's okay in its place," I replied. "There was a little of that in the ATC, and I liked it. Liked it even more at summer camp. Things are pretty cut and fucking dried in the Air Force—let's face it, there's something a bit more honest about being highly organized in order to bloody well kill people than there is about being regimented—mentally—to look down on them. 'Them' being those insignificant types who didn't get into a 'good' school."

"You were talking about not belonging," said Joy.

"I didn't know I'd stopped."

"Oh, come on, John. Let's skip the tangents."

"Oh, very well. So—most of the time I can live with it. But whenever I'm somewhere where I know. Or feel. I just don't belong. I never have the sense to simply leave. Case in point—kind of—a couple of weeks ago."

"Oh, really?" said Joy. "I'm not sure I'm all ears. But you may as well tell me."

I gulped.

"Okay," I said. "I was out with some—er—bright young things. And hanging out in particular with someone I happen to like, okay, a little more than I should. Sonia. The woman I took to La Capeline, as it happens. She comes from, oh, a fair bit of money. Okay, so I'm married. But the liking is mutual. So she likes me, a little more than she should—maybe—since she's engaged. So there we were at a gig, at some jazz club. (Her fiancé, Simon, who's a very nice bloke, was working.) And the big man in the headline act—guy called Billy, plays sax—is a friend of hers. And he's also a fucking good sculptor, makes a very comfortable living at it. So she introduced me after the show. Which was fine. But, a few minutes later, she was off in a huddle with her girlfriends. And I was nursing a twelve-dollar glass of Sancerre. And the big man walks over and gets me alone and says, 'So you're the married English prick Sonia's always talking about. The working-class asshole with the so-called classical education. Am I right? Well, listen up, fuckhead. If Simon wasn't around, and *you* were in the running, I'd do everything I fucking could to talk her out of it. And I'll tell you why. Because you don't deserve her.'"

"That was bloody rude," said Joy. "So what did you say?"

"Nothing. Absolutely nothing. Something inside me said: 'Guess what—he's right.' So I said goodnight to Sonia, and I scarpered. Feeling so fucked I couldn't be bothered to catch a cab or take the bloody subway. So I walked across the bridge."

"Are you out of your mind?" said Joy. "Don't you know a toad when you see one?"

"I'm sorry," I said. "But the bastard really got to me. I just felt so hobbled—and haunted. Actually, it's worse than that: I felt defined. By what? The piss-poor stories. Way back when. And now, what with Mum's situation, and Dad's. He didn't live well those last few years, stuck in a virtual bedsit and putting up with a roommate."

"You're being completely unrealistic," said Joy. "I know what I said about KEGS and all that, a moment ago. But this stuff, John—you're just too vulnerable to it."

"Do you think I don't know that?" I said. "I can't help it. And that makes it ten times worse."

—

THE WEEK THAT FOLLOWED was my idea of idyllic. Sadness was tempered by fonder memories, and Joy and I grew closer than ever. She fed me massive quantities of expertly prepared vegetarian food and never complained when I disappeared to dispose of a sausage or two within sight of the paint cans. And on the eve of my departure, she prepared two kinds of bangers (fake for her, pork of the pigtail genus for me) with onion gravy and plain mashed potatoes, opened a bottle of Viognier, rolled herself a cigarette, and scorched it.

"Aren't we going to eat?" I tinkled, mindlessly parking my half-empty glass on a much-thumbed copy of the Peter Green translation of Ovid's poems of exile.

"Of course we are. But the food's a bit hot. And so is the house. And I know how much you like a fag with your very first glug of the evening."

"And not just the first glug," I gargled, unpacking a Camel. "As you know."

"It's been lovely having you over. I'm sorry I couldn't get more time off work."

"No need to worry about that. I know how to enjoy myself here. Especially in the summer. Sit in the park and read—without critiquing. I hardly ever get time for personal reading back home. Except on the subway, of course. It blocks out the horror show."

"So," said Joy. "Back to New York tomorrow. How are you coping over there? Really?"

"With what?" I asked. "Life in general? Losing Dad? The impending separation—well, 'separate living arrangements' is how Pam puts it. Life at *Gourmet?*"

"Losing Dad, for a start. *And* the separation."

"On the Dad front," I said. "About as well as you. Water-logged for the rest of my natural life. Losing Dad made me look at everything, including the stuff I was on about down at the caff."

"It was bound to," she said.

"So. You know. Displaced. Much more displaced than when Dad was alive."

"Oh."

"The pleb in the palazzo. At Condé Nast and elsewhere. Or, as I once said to Dad, the bumpkin in the ballroom."

"He mentioned that to me," said Joy. "He seemed a bit upset about it. Said he'd come to think of you as a very good mixer, good at getting on with all kinds of people."

"He wasn't completely off the mark," I said. "And I'm sorry he was upset. But I never had the heart to tell him ex-actly what it was costing me at times. The walking on eggshells. What to say, what not to say. How to invent a ve-neer of—what? Sophistication? How to do poise when scared shitless, without being seen through. How to play the gentle-man, when I'm not."

"Oh, come on," said Joy. "Depends on what you mean by 'gentleman.' I wouldn't call you *too* lost a cause on that score."

"I would," I said. "So there I am. Behold the man. Now in New York. Born in Romford. Barely escaped growing up—meaning 'down,' as Mum knew very well—in bloody Rain-ham. And now, developing what I believe they call taste. Dinners for two that cost as much as—what?—fish and chips for fifty in Brixton or Woodford. Pissing away more wine in a week than Dad ever drank in a year. And then there's the music: out goes Eric Clapton, in comes Carla Bley. But the worst thing is, there's this really awful downside. Something I need to be careful about—I hope you don't mind my wittering on like this?"

"You obviously need to," said Joy, lighting another cigarette. "So what is it? This thing you need to be careful about?"

"Well," I said. "I've been told I'm becoming stuck-up."

"That's ridiculous," said Joy.

"I'd have thought so, too," I said, "until a couple of months ago. I was out for a drink with a female friend who works at *The Wall Street Journal*. And at one point she said— and I've absolutely no idea what I'd said—'You can be a bit of a snob at times, John.' That kept me quiet for a bit. Very bloody quiet indeed."

"That's so strange," said Joy. "Did she bother to tell you why she thought that?"

"No," I said. "She didn't. She's really nice, by the way. And the worst thing is, if anyone's entitled to spot a snob, it's her."

"How come?"

"Gina," I said, "is very working-class. And very hardheaded. And unlike a lot of people I now know over there, she had to work a full-time job, more or less, all the way through college. As, too, did Pam, as it happens."

"I see," said Joy. "But I still can't quite believe it."

"Maybe it's because you hardly ever see me on my home turf," I said. "I don't know."

"Well, if it's true, I'm surprised."

"You aren't the only one. I hate to think what Dad would say."

"He'd be a bit bemused."

"And then," I said, "to make things worse, Sonia gave me a similar earful—sort of—a few weeks later, at a *Gourmet* after-party I'd dragged her along to."

"Oh, dear. Maybe you should avoid those."

"I've thought about that. And—well—decided not to. They're too much fun. So—Sonia, who was privately educated at staggering expense all the way from kindergarten through grad school, and has a conservative streak a mile wide, but can also be a crazy woman, stopped me and said: 'You know what, John Haney? I think you're a man of extremes with just enough of a sense of decorum to keep you out of trouble.' "

Joy smirked. "How badly were you misbehaving?"

"I wasn't misbehaving at all. I can play a very straight game even when I'm totally fucking smashed. But she and I are pretty good friends, like I said, and she's kind of astute. And she's also seen the English working class in action in half the pubs in Norwich. Friend of hers from college lives there now. And there you have it."

"Have what?" said Joy.

"Still a bit of a boor from backwoods Ongar, if Sonia's to be believed. But also, according to Gina, a bit stuck-up. So maybe I've been—and always will be—both things. Maybe there *is* a bit of Ongar that stayed inside me, and bloody well won't get lost—like all those bits of German steel that ended up living in Grandpa. My dullard side. The one I have to watch whenever I'm out and about with the beautiful people. And maybe there's a bit of KEGS that just won't go away. . . . Hmmm, that reminds me: remember that time Jeremy Jones popped over to Ongar with a bloke called Leonard? Younger kid from KEGS who was thinking of applying to Royal Holloway?"

"Vaguely," said Joy. "I was always pleased to see Jeremy. One of the very few nice blokes you were at school with."

"Oh, yes. Always the gentleman. And he still is. They don't take yobs in the Anglican clergy. Anyway, you were in the front room, reading Ibsen and looking steamy. And the three of us came wandering back from the Stag with a couple of pints inside us."

"I rather doubt that," said Joy. "The 'steamy' bit, that is. And I don't remember the Ibsen."

"Are you kidding?" I said. "You were all skintight jeans and bare shoulders. I thought Lennie was going to wet himself. He went completely bloody bug-eyed. And after I'd introduced you and you'd gone off to read *The Wild Duck* somewhere else and after I'd told him how much drunken fun I was having at RHC, he says: 'Your sister. She's, er, very pretty.' And I said: 'Right first time, Lennie. Alpha fucking plus for observation.' 'Where does she go to school?' he asked. 'Just up the road,' I replied. 'Ongar Comprehensive.' 'Oh,' he said, 'I see. Didn't it used to be a secondary modern?' Bloody well lost interest immediately. Which, I think, would not have been the case if you'd been at the Ursuline in Brentwood or that very nice grammar school for a better class of tart in—where was it?—Loughton. The one that Vicki went to."

"Well, like I said," sighed Joy, who now seemed depressed, "there was Jeremy, the gentleman. And half a dozen others, including you, who could just about behave themselves without being told to. And then there was everybody else."

"Thanks a lot," I said. "And getting back to Lennie. I honestly felt like throwing him out. And maybe giving him a very swift kick up the arse for fucking good measure. But I didn't. You know what that means? I excused him. I might just as well have stood there and said: 'Go ahead, Lennie. Belittle my sister. You won't hear a peep out of me. After all. We have both worn the same fucking cap, the same fucking tie, and the same fucking stupid blazer.' "

"I don't think it means you excused his behavior," said Joy. "And you'll just have to learn to deal with these 'downsides.' Gina's probably right. And as for your 'inner boor,' Sonia could be right, too. She probably finds it exotic. Just keep them both at bay, for God's sake. The 'downsides,' I mean, not your friends. It shouldn't be too hard."

"I hope not," I said. "Who knows? Maybe they'll die of neglect."

"Doesn't everything?" said Joy.

"Yes, I guess everything does. Which brings us, I suppose, to my domestic situation. Things have been neglected there—and I honestly feel that neither of us could help it."

"I'm worried sick about this," said Joy. "I still can't bloody understand exactly how this whole disaster is working. So you have your problems. We can't deny that—"

"We shouldn't."

"—and it's driving Pam crazy. And she's also saying she needs her own space. She told me that herself. And I'm terribly fond of her, terribly fond. But—are those two things *actually* related?"

"I just don't know. I just don't bloody know. But we are a long way, a fucking long way, up shit creek. So bloody far that it's almost as if the reasons, whatever they might be, no longer matter. The situation is what it is. And both of us are miserable. Utterly bloody miserable."

"Could it be the New York effect? Trying to live a normal life in fuck-all space?"

"But Pam and I are living in a loft. Though we're sharing it with her business. Which happens to make economic sense."

"Well, if you ask me, it's also part of the problem. A big part."

"I'm sorry," I said. "I refuse to be that ungenerous. It obviously doesn't bloody help. But that's life: rarely convenient."

"But how will you cope, living alone for the first time in your life? I mean, you went straight from Number 13 to the Cheshire Home. Surrounded by people. Then to college— same goes there. Then to Brixton. Then to Pam. You know, loneliness has been clinically proven not to be good for your health. Mental or physical."

"I'll have to get used to it, won't I? And try to get myself straightened out somehow. I won't be the first bloke who's been in this boat, you know."

"Well, I'm sorry, John. And I hate to say this. But I think Pam's taking a bit of a risk with these 'separate living arrangements.' "

"I think I'll manage to behave myself. I'm not a complete bloody animal, you know. Party animal sometimes, sure. But I've never laid a finger on Sonia."

"I'm sure you haven't. But that was then, John. I'm concerned about now. And you're the one who's moving out. How are you supposed to get better when you've had to leave home?"

"I don't know. I'll just have to do my best, Joy, won't I? Other people have coped."

"I'm not so sure about that. This all seems like—like— I don't know, going from the frying pan straight to the fire."

"You could be right. But Pam deserves some happiness, too. I can be impossible to live with. Absolutely impossible."

"You're being too nice. This all feels a bit bloody lose-lose to me."

"Maybe it is. But whatever happens, I happen to love Pam dearly. Maybe there is a way back. Like I said, we'll just have to see."

"Not much else we can do, is there?"

"No."

Neither of us spoke for several minutes.

"Maybe it's time to change the subject," I sighed. "So— er—this probably sounds like a frivolous question right now . . . but I was wondering, What are we having for lunch tomorrow?"

THE ANSWER to that question came in the form of a meal we put together as a reasonably authentic re-creation of a repast we had frequently eaten as children at teatime, out in the garden, on Sundays in June, July, August, and (weather permitting) September. Joy avoided the meat, of course, but appreciated the historical accuracy of the pile of cold baked ham and the hatbox of a pork pie (with a hard-boiled egg imprisoned at its core) that I had purchased at the super-market that morning. Also on the menu were good crisp let-tuce, stinging spring onions, cold new potatoes, and dollops of a mayonnaise (organic) that bore a blessedly striking resemblance, both in taste and in texture, to Heinz Salad Cream.

After we'd finished, we sat and smoked in silence for several minutes, taking turns to tickle Horace (Joy's alarmingly globular cat) and topping up our tea.

"That's funny," I said.

"What?" said Joy.

"I can smell cigar smoke. And kippers. It's faint, but—oh, maybe not. It's gone now."

"That happened to me once, last summer. The cigar smoke, not the kippers. At Jackie's. In her bedroom. We'd just done some laundry and I was . . . putting away some sheets. And it hit me, like Saturday afternoons at 207. So I opened the windows. Wasn't thinking, really. It was strange."

"I'll say it's strange," I said. "Still, must have been something I ate. Probably the scallions. Or maybe the new potatoes."

"And maybe it wasn't," said Joy.

"Oh, I see," I said. "Grandpa's ghost. Just couldn't bear to leave Beehive Lane. And sometimes takes the bus to Crystal Palace."

"Well, it gave *me* the shivers, a bit."

"I'm sure it did. But it's probably best not to panic. That was a very authentic salad, you know. We deserve a prize for that. Just like the old days. Which I do sometimes find myself missing."

"I know you do," said Joy. "You were miles away at one point."

"Oh really?" I said. "And which point was that?"

"Oh . . ." said Joy, "you were just about to eat a new potato, actually. And you stopped. Funny. I thought you were crying for a minute. I don't know why I thought that. I mean—well, you weren't."

"Maybe I should have been," I said.

"What do you mean?" said Joy, rather sadly.

"Better out than in, I suppose," I replied. "In the long run. Really. You know, ever since I got back to New York after Dad died, I've wanted to cry, and I couldn't. 'Look—no tears.' Just wouldn't come. Still felt like shit. Awful, really awful—everything about bloody crying, except the tears. When it gets really bad, I end up gasping for breath. Gasping. Which makes it even worse."

"Oh," said Joy. "Yes. Yes, it would."

"Maybe it's because I wasn't there," I said, "that I still sometimes find myself wondering, trying to guess. And a very poorly educated guess that would be. How his last few minutes must have looked. I just have this, oh, horrible suspicion that—well. Having to fight for every breath would keep you awake—wide awake. Until you took your last one. And at first I thought, when the tears wouldn't come, Oh, this must mean that what they call the healing has begun. And then I thought, No, it bloody hasn't, and it never bloody will. Because he's in me. He hasn't 'gone' anywhere. And especially not to Upminster. He's in me. Forever. And so will Mum and Jackie be when they go. And Rose. And Ray. Everyone. So this is where they've been going when they've bloody well gone and copped it. Nana Haney. Dave Dick Joan. Eileen Ena. Don. Grandma Bush. And Grandpa. And maybe that's what stops me from being too much of a snob—or a yob."

"Possibly," said Joy. She rolled another cigarette.

"You know, I really was hoping, in some ways, that the

healing might have begun. But perhaps that's a selfish position to take. Does that sound crazy? Maybe I'm actually better off without the bloody healing. What if the healing involves forgetting? Why would I want to forget all the things that made me what I am? Maybe it's best to keep the sores open, but clean. To let all those deaths go on hurting. And the lives that came before them go on being a part of mine. No matter how insignificant and—well, quite frequently—sad they were. Maybe that's where I do belong. And maybe I should stop trying to belong . . . somewhere else. The next rung up the ladder. This is me, Joy—what we just ate. And this is me, too. Here with you. As close to being home again as I'm ever going to get."

"Really?" said Joy.

"Yes, really. I'm actually beginning to think that, after all these years away, I could never be a part of England again—not in the here and now. And I honestly don't feel at home in America. The way I remember—at one time—I felt at home here. But England remembered—as I experienced it—is better than no bloody England at all. I can't write all these memories off as something like an illusion. There's nothing insubstantial about what Grandpa went through. Or about bangers. Or the complications—the fucking interminable complications—of class."

"I'm always here for you, John," said Joy. "I suppose I always have been. Even when we were barely talking. From the time I went to the Dump until I passed some exams you . . . respected. And when I was at the commune, which you just didn't get. It was what we had in common that counted. Meaning Dad. And Mum. I know you've had—and

still have—a difficult relationship with her. A lot more difficult than mine. But it won't be a picnic when she goes either.
Just different."

"I know you're here for me," I said. "I have noticed."

"Even when you're miles away." She sniffed—then
smiled. "Literally, and when you're dreaming. So—where
exactly were you? When you gave that potato a break?"

"A lifetime away. And not just my own. Lifetimes, then.
All those others."

"But where exactly? I'm curious."

"Several places at once, if you must know."

"As always."

"Yes. Quite. As always. Why am I suddenly reminded of
an Army joke?"

"God knows," said Joy. "Seems a little apropos of nothing."

"You think so? It was one of Dad's favorites. All fucking
hell breaking loose. Every poor bugger scared shitless. And
some wag says: 'Cheer up, lads. It could be worse. At least it
isn't raining.' "

"Hmmm. That's a good one," said Joy. "But it wasn't my
favorite. I liked the one about the message that got garbled
when they passed it down the line."

"Oh, yes," I smiled wanly. " 'Send for reinforcements—
we're going to advance.' Which turned into—"

" 'Lend us three and fourpence—we're going to a
dance.' "

"Is there any tea left?"

"I'll make some," she said, then paused. "I was actually
thinking of Grandpa just the other day. Thinking that the

days I remember most clearly were when it was raining. And I sometimes think that whenever it rained at Grandpa's there was—really—no rain quite like it."

"I felt that sometimes," I said. "And it made him so depressed."

"Probably reminded him of all the bloody times he'd had to fight in it."

"Mum said something like that to me, just before I left England. In a Pizza Express, of all places."

"Come to think of it," said Joy. "Grandpa's house was, well, always a bit cheerless, even in summer. And yet you and I did have some happy times there."

"I know we did," I said. "But I sometimes think the undercurrent is something we're still waking up to. Though God knows it should have been obvious. How could the hell he went through not have colored—tainted—overshadowed—everything? All of us?"

"Of course it did," said Joy. "We had no choice in the matter."

"And there we have it."

"Have what?"

"Grandpa's legacy—sausages and sadness."

"That's one way of looking at it," said Joy. "But can we go back to that question I asked you?"

"Oh yes," I said, lighting another cigarette and inhaling hard. "Where was I? Thinking about some recently rediscovered emotional milestones. Not just the ones I mentioned to you after Don died."

"Huh?" said Joy.

"You know. The Vulcan. Making love to Helen. Don's party. North Weald."

"Oh."

"Things have changed a lot. A fuck of a lot. With Dad gone."

"It's the same for me, too."

"I know it is."

Silence fell, deepened, resurrected the feeling of timelessness, of time having stopped, that had struck me as I sat in the funeral parlor and stared at a shabby cadaver with a cactus for a nose.

"So—the potato," I muttered, stubbing out the cigarette and slightly burning a buttery thumb and two fingers in the process. "I'll tell you exactly where I was when I gave it a little stay of execution. I don't think you'll be too surprised."

IT WAS, ALWAYS will be, and always is quite late on a cricket-pocked afternoon in the west half of Essex, midsummer, circa 1964. My mother's garden gently seeps a Ladybird book's worth of luminous flowers: Arabis, Aubretia, late hyacinths, Sweet William, delphiniums, pinks, stocks, dimwit hollyhocks, and, last and least, a sullen reef of psychically defeated antirrhinums. The vegetable patch, soon past its best, sends out: slug pellets, runner beans, chicken wire, kitchen string, charcoals of rhubarb, temperas of carrots, liverish abstracts of onions. Two cats refuse to be hurried. They decompose in a yard of clay beneath a leafy overcast of effervescent apples. A third, alive but far from well, its larynx a windfall of blisters, looks sinfully proud of the sparrow it's killed but can't eat. (This, I remember, is Twinkle.) A rabbit, less damaged, grows bored ignored, whiffles and whumps in its hutch. (That's Thumper.) A forepaw of butterflies—admirals, turtleshells, creosote whites, cabbage sky-blues, and small coppers—flit-flaps open, snaps clam-shut, and glares at the lawn from the rockery. The indigenous crows (rooks to all speakers of English) are racketing home to a shock-headed stand of immovable elms and to the sound of every last bell of our wristful of Anglican churches. Evensong, it gleams, is now upon us.

In neighboring gardens, certain sights, certain sounds. Cutlery clinks on cheap china. (Except, it must be said, at Auntie Jennifer's.) Teaspoons clonk in tiresome mugs, seducing cube sugar and cow juice to tingles of sweet milky tea. Joy and I are sitting on the backdoor steps, next to an aquarium of tadpoles. At our feet, respectively, a sketch book and *The Hobbit*. A hedgehog—it's sick, we think—meanders on the patio, decrying all small frogs, belated assistance, ignoring a slippage of souring milk in a well-intentioned saucer. My father, a pea-knotted shirt and preposterous tie, is biting his tongue in a hurry before leaving home for a night shift. Mum gently asks if we (Joy and I) want any more before she starts putting the leftovers into our *Guardian*-overgrown fridge, a sated white leech living next to the counter, where bread crumbs are breeding like warts.

My sister, a daydream, says nothing, a non-modulation of hush. I, on the other hand—as became, I now recalled, a human flea who could always be relied upon to hop like one demented when the dinner bell yelled "Biscuit tin!" (and the asphalt clanged to the restive clucks of an underweight brigade of starving infants streaking across the playground to a paradise on earth where the manna came from a mutton shop and the angels had strawberry faces and blubbery arms)—can hear myself saying: "A bit more ham, please, Mum."

Next I saw sludge, a small ocean of mud. Smudge between fields and the sea. A man with a boat and two children. And, from a floodgate, protectively waving, his wife, in a sundress: a worry, a flurry, a panic-prone dot, a disquieted dash of multi-colored mail-order cotton. The man's wife. Their mother. But muted: by the breeze, stillborn water, the underworld weight of the child she miscarried (as I learned at fifteen) a year or so before I was expelled from a comfortable bloodbath and held upside down in the air. Mum. In a sundress. Encircled by sun-dials and warmly besieged by the mystical blitter of birds.

There followed my sister and me. On a frigid village evening worthy of Gogol's Dikanka. Infuriate imp of just-turned-three, white-knuckled goblin of five, squabbling over our rocking horse in the sickening glint of a fizz fight of grumbledown coals. Just feet away, Dad. Odor-burdened, radiating: carbon paper, two-star petrol, drip-dry shirts, spilt milk, and sugared almonds; Wonder Bread, weed killer, cheese, electricity, axle grease, Woodford, and gravy; teleprinters, fiberglass, Ovaltine, anthracite, cornstarch, and stunted sat-sumas. Dad—a single-handed slave to the sticky-floored cat flap that passed for his kitchen, warming the teapot, stoking the boiler, hovering over half-cooked eggs, loosening the lid of the Marmite jar, cracking down hard on clumped-up salt, debating whether or not to tell his kids to knock it off.

Last, before I reemerged—into South London sunshine, Joy's quizzical silence, my stillness, the scent of container-grown flowers—I caught a vicarious glimpse and first sight of a corpse going cold, like an overlooked meal, in a cupboard.

The corpse of a kind man who was, in his own way, in many ways wise and his wisdoms remind me, whenever I'm swept up in dimly lit outpours of eye-searing linen and crystal, that long before his son maintained a taste for tartares and Clos Blanc de Vougeot, there lived and teethed a little boy who "quite liked" a kipper and drank pints of cocoa and was partial to poached eggs with buttercup fins and strangely enamored of custard.

Ham and Cheese, Egg Salad,
Ham Solitaire

. . . .

EARLY IN JANUARY 2006, OVERWHELMED BY LONELINESS AND, to my despair, no longer feeling able to ignore an increasing sense of irreparable estrangement, I told Pam, with regret, that I wanted to separate formally. A few days later, Mum suffered a catastrophic stroke, went into a coma, and lasted for almost a month. Over that time, Joy and Pip scuttled back and forth between Norfolk and London to the point of sheer exhaustion, dividing their time in Norwich between sitting at her bedside and, having been assured that Mum would not recover, emptying her flat (in the few days allowed for the task by the housing association) of hundreds of books, numerous shopping bags jam-packed with newspaper clippings (mostly from the *Guardian*), and the avalanche of shop-bought cakes and antiquated biscuits that had greeted Joy when she set about disposing of the contents of Mum's kitchen cupboards.

Mum in Norwich, November 2005

The funeral was a simple affair, attended only by Pip and Joy. (Jackie was too frail to travel.) A wake, which I attended, was held in March at Mum's favorite tearoom and attracted roughly twenty of her friends, including the secretary of the Norwich Humanist Society, her Age Concern case worker, and a slightly eccentric young woman named Nina, whom she had met only two weeks before she collapsed. Nina, despite being wheelchair-bound with early-stage multiple sclerosis, turned a small portion of the afternoon into a *thé à musique* and a tribute to Mum's harmonic predilections by playing (competently, to my sincere relief) Debussy's "Syrinx" on the flute and then singing (a cappella) Holst's "The Heart Worships."

I knew almost nobody there and preferred—what with debilitating jet lag and the leaden sensation making ever deeper inroads into the muddle of muscle and fat repeating itself mere inches from my ribs—not to mingle. Instead, I restrained my gaze to the panoply of sandwiches (ham and cheese, egg salad, ham solitaire, something that might have been salmon) and three kinds of cake (slightly dry chocolate, concrete fruit, and almond) on offer and to photographs of Mum that Joy had retrieved from moth-beaten albums and boxes. Kitty at the age of ten or thereabouts, half-smiling, painfully shy. With Dad on honeymoon in Bournemouth.

Mum picking grapes on Chios, 1986

Mum on honeymoon, 1950

With Jackie, in a half-lit crowd, on VJ Day in Redbridge. With Roger, in the early days, the two of them dressed like aging hippies (which, in some ways, they were) and sitting, not too elegantly, in the wreckage of a haystack. Picking grapes on a cooperative farm on Chios in 1986. With Pam and me in Lincoln's Inn Fields shortly before the Mono-chrome Set released their second album.

During the drive back to London the following day, Joy and Pip and I, wrestling with the *Guardian*'s least difficult crossword, spent several minutes on a clue whose solution en-tailed reproducing the first half-line of a poem by Dylan Thomas.

"Bugger," said Joy. "I just don't get it. "'Gently' isn't working."

"Well, it bloody well should be," I said. "Everybody—including Rodney Dangerfield—knows this one."

"I wonder if it's their mistake," said Joy.

"Unfortunately, I doubt it."

"Got it!" said Pip. "It's 'gentle,' not 'gently.' "

"I can't believe we got that wrong," I muttered. "So—is that it?"

"Yes," said Joy. "And the whole annoying thing only took the three of us an hour."

"That," I said—reopening a Penguin selection of very short pieces by Kafka and wondering if "Josephine the Singer,

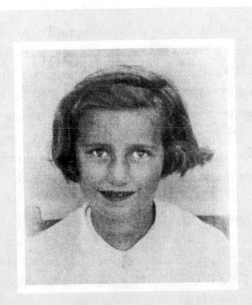

Mum in 1940

or the Mouse-folk" would venture as close to neurosis as "Wedding Preparations in the Country"—"is flat-out shameful. Time for a cigarette break, I think. Can we pull over? I'm gasping."

(Smoking in the car was not permitted. Pip hadn't smoked for more than a decade at this point, and Joy, to my horror, had been nicotine-free for two years and was still slightly niggled by my tongue-in-cheek contention, which I'd offered when she quit, that renouncing tobacco would cost her what little was left of her working-class credentials.)

"No problem," said Pip.

Sullenly eyeing a sodden field and a sad-looking cow a few miles from Ipswich some five minutes later, I took a first shiver-shocked nip at a Camel and suddenly heard the determined approach of the one-note whistle I'd originally come to revel in while smearing clots of Clearasil onto unstoppable acne in barrack blocks in Cornwall and the Midlands.

"Christ! Fuck!" Pip squawked in awe as a thunderclap scream and its earsplitting shadow announced the near overhead passage at speed of a composite tonnage of hard-charging airframe cunningly attached to a heartless duet of high-performance engines. "He's flying a bit bloody low."

"Are they allowed to do that?" Joy spluttered.

"Probably not in this neck of the woods," I coughed, oddly entranced by the flood of manure that had just begun to cascade from the apparently uninterested cow and belatedly wondering, nevertheless, if the plane had been a Harrier or a Tornado. "But if I was driving one of those things, it's just what I'd do for a lark."

The fact that, for once, I'd failed to look up when for a

matter of moments mere yards from a low-flying military aircraft was something that Joy, not surprisingly, noticed.

"My God," she said. "I've never seen you so—so indifferent."

"Just not in the mood today, quite frankly. Can't believe Mum's dead. It's stupid, I know."

"Neither can I."

"Did I ever tell you I got to talk to Matthew when Jane went?" I asked. Jane Burgess had died of pneumonia in 1997, having outlived her husband by three years.

"No."

"Mum gave him my number. First time we'd talked in twenty years. Fuck me, it's cold. And, well, he said that with both parents gone, it was like he'd had some cosmic rug pulled right out from under him. And I think that's how this feels. Surprised me, though. Coming from Matthew. The latter-day Matthew. Hard-headed bloke with a wife and three kids. And a serious career. You know he left Cambridge? Got a hot job in the private sector. Doing weird things to wheat, I think. Kind of stuff we worry about at *Gourmet*." (The cow, to my consternation, was still producing.)

"I'm sure there's still some softie left in Matthew," said Joy. "Remember those stupid boxing lessons Julian made him take? To toughen him up?"

"Oh, yes," I said. "They didn't work. I mean, okay, he wasn't exactly the Basher type. But he wasn't a *total* weakling."

"I could use a cigarette today," sniffed Joy. "I really could."

"I'm sure you could," I said coldly, flicking my dog end

into a ditch and coming to the conclusion that the cow was in need of a vet.

"Appetite's gone to pieces."

"Yeah, well, mine's not what it was before Mum went, either. They ain't gettin' much money out of me these days in the Condé Nast cafeteria."

"Still haven't been there, you know."

"Okay, okay—next time you're over. I promise."

"I suppose we'll have to eat something tonight."

"Too bloody right," said Pip. "Got to keep the old strength up."

"Yeah. Well. Whatever," I said. "No need to bash your brains out, Joy."

"I couldn't."

"I know what I probably could force down," I said, brushing imaginary cat hair (Horace's) from my trousers.

"What?"

"A marmalade sandwich."

"PRETTY BAD TIMING, wasn't it?" said Joy as the car sped south past Chelmsford. "For you, I mean. Mum dying when she did. So soon after the breakup with Pam."

"Wasn't exactly ideal," I replied. "Kind of got me thinking again. That it might have been my grieving for Dad that went and tipped the balance for the marriage."

"That had occurred to me," said Joy. "And maybe having to do the grieving such a long way from home. And on your own, unfortunately. For the last four years."

"Hmmm. As if the depression and drinking weren't bad enough. Sling in some grief—that'll be nice. Not really."

"No," said Joy. "Not really."

"You know, Pam sometimes says she feels she and I have been defeated by circumstances."

"I can see her point. But, well, right now you are where you are. And I get to worry about you. All over again. The way I did five years ago. Just before you moved out."

"I wouldn't worry too much. Sure, it looks awful. Well— not just looks. It is bloody awful. Complete fucking mess. But I'll manage."

"I hope so."

"Guess I'll go the Dad route. Keep your head down. Just keep going. Just . . . keep . . . fucking . . . going. 'Remember, son, there's always someone much worse off than you.' "

"Will you cope?"

"I'll have to."

"A girlfriend might help."

"Won't be going there for a while. Not unless someone who finds me utterly irresistible—because she's into basket cases—turns up out of the blue. Not until I've begun to re- cover from both shocks. Wouldn't be fair on the other person. But I have been trying to get out more. Which just got a little bit easier, thank God, thanks to something called Copy Drinks."

"What's that?"

"Oh, sort of a networking thing. Woman at one of the other Condé Nast mags dreamed it up. So once a month the word nerds, as we call ourselves, descend on a bar on the Lower East Side. For a fairly civilized piss-up. And a chat. It's okay."

"Really?"

"Better than nothing. Better than sitting at home in an

empty apartment. And one thing leads to another sometimes. Which brings me back to coping, believe it or not."

"Really?"

"Yes. Thanks to a handful of those folks, I ended up going to a reading at this crazy antique of a bar on the Brooklyn waterfront. Bit of a dive. But a nice dive. Been there forever. And the moment I walked in, I wondered whether Grandpa had known it, back in his days with Cunard."

"Interesting thought."

"Got me thinking. So that was a Sunday afternoon, the Sunday after Mum keeled over. And things got pretty convivial after the readings. And I felt—well—quite comfortable. And not too dreadful. Which I hope doesn't sound *too* fucking thoughtless. What with Mum in intensive care and attached to all kinds of machines, and you and Pip doing the headless chicken."

"It's not a bit thoughtless. For God's sake, John. I'm glad you had a nice time."

"Anyway. There was this one woman in the little crowd that I was hanging out with who had the most *extraordinary* sense of humor. Completely fucking hilarious. Really, really witty."

"Has she got a boyfriend?" Joy glinted.

"Yes," I said. "And he was looking extremely pleased with himself, as he should be. Don't get your hopes up there, love."

"Just trying to help."

"I know. And I'd been sitting there thinking how—the joint we were in. If you ripped out the bar, and all the banquettes, it wouldn't be a whole lot different from all the dingy village halls and community halls where we went to weddings and parties. And then she said something completely ridiculous. What was it? Something about the high demand for Astroglide and Ex-Lax among middle-aged Republican women. Well, that got us laughing. Yes, we were drunk. And maybe it wasn't that funny, maybe it was just the way she said it. But I was howling. Honestly. Howling. The way I did at Nana jokes—you know: 'I'm not moving for that bastard Hitler.' I went blue in the face over that one. And, as Mum once reminded me, sneezed a cup of tea all over you."

"I've forgotten that."

"It brought the bloody house down, believe me. So that was when the ghosts walked in—reeking of winkles and whiskey. And seeing them all again like that. Imagining them. These people I loved, and who gives a flying fuck how fucked-up some of them—two of them—were? It really felt good. But the weird thing is, Dick and Joan were really well defined."

"What's weird about that?"

"Isn't it obvious? They had a problem—you know. The one I've got now."

"I don't think you're as badly off as they were, John. Honestly."

"Let's hope not. So anyway. I guess. At that moment— and just for a moment, even with Mum in the state she was in and you in sheer hell and the marriage in fucking ruins— I was almost as happy as I'd ever been. I mean, when I was a child. The laughter I was hearing—in the real world—it seemed to be echoing theirs. So I still have all that to fall back on. The people who made me. The Haney mob entire. Even though we hardly ever saw them and they're all fucking dead now. Well, not quite all. And then—of course—there's Dad."

"There's always Dad."

"Soldiering on. With Bren gun and briefcase. Soldiering on and on and on. I think I'll be okay."

"I hope so. I just feel so helpless. When you're so unhappy, and so far away."

"Really, Joy—I'll be fine. A woman I used to work with—English as it happens—retired now—edited anything *Gourmet* got from Julian Barnes and Jan Morris—she said that once she'd lost both parents she had this sense of new horizons opening up. Because the change was. Well—so fundamental."

"Sounds a bit optimistic to me, just now."

I ignored her.

"So who knows?" I swept on. "New relationship? Maybe. A long way—a very long way—down the road. But why not new friendships? Most of the friends I do have began life as Pam's. And no one's taking sides, thank God. But new friends. Under my own steam. That'd be good. And I've just begun going to church again."

"Bloody hell. Nothing fundamentalist, I hope."

"Of course not. Episcopal—Anglican. A very progressive congregation. All persuasions. Sex-wise. Faith-wise. In well-heeled Brooklyn Heights."

" 'In man's extremity . . .' "

" '. . . is God's opportunity.' Who the hell told you that one?"

"Jeremy. The weekend he was my escort for your last Summer Ball at RHC."

"I can't believe he was preaching to you. Wasn't exactly his style with the nonbelievers."

"Jeremy wasn't preaching to me. We'd just had a hell of a lot to drink. Not as much as you, of course . . ."

"Thanks a lot," I muttered, remembering how my approach to paralysis (six pints of Heineken, two Black Russians, a couple of glasses of Beaujolais, and a bottle of bogus champagne) had earned me a verbal kicking from an extremely upset and (for the moment and quite justifiably) sex-denying and full-bore hysterical Helen.

". . . and I liked him. A lot. I was curious about his decision to try for the priesthood."

"Interesting. Anyway. Things aren't *that* bad. I am not in extremity yet. And I'm also thinking of tarting up my French."

"Why not?"

"Alliance Française. Something like that. Knowing a few French food terms doesn't get you all that far if you suddenly feel the need to read a fucking great lump of Flaubert's correspondence. In the original. So we'll see. I know it seems piecemeal."

"What?"

"Getting out more. Going to church. Brushing up the Frog. Not exactly a master plan. But a new life has to start somewhere. And, frankly, I bloody well need one."

"POOR RAY," SAID JOY, some time later, as the Volvo skirted Stratford—sunk beneath a winter sky that reminded me of ice-cold late-autumnal afternoons part-spent aboard the Pre-

fect on our customarily carsick way to Grandpa's. "I think he
felt a bit lost, being the last of the Haney boys. He called me
every Christmas after Dad died."

Ray had been dead for two years. Jackie and Rose were
now the sole survivors of their generation of the families.

"Know what Ray told me the last time I called him?" I
said. "If it wasn't for Dad, he'd never have snagged that job
with the Inland Revenue. He'd missed so much school with
his migraines—I wonder if *that* was down to malnutrition?—
he left knowing nothing. Or next to nothing. So Dad taught
him maths when he had the time. And helped him with his
English. Whenever he was home on leave. And for a little bit
after the war."

"Really?" said Joy. "Gosh—that reminds me of some-

With Mum, 1954

thing Mum's friend Jennie said. You know, her best friend. Who lived on the council estate."

"I remember Jennie."

"I called to tell her Mum had gone. And she said. If it wasn't for Mum. She would never—literally never—have read a book. It was Mum who got her reading. Lent her *On the Beach*."

"DO YOU THINK Mum went 'gentle'?" asked Joy as the Crystal Palace transmission mast swam into view.

"Oh, I shouldn't think so," I said. "I'm sure she had one last 'pissed-off pensioner' letter to write when her poor old brain exploded. Or some riveting documentary she simply couldn't *wait* to watch on Channel Four."

"Well, I need to believe she went gentle," said Joy. "At the very end. Just for once. I mean, maybe being gentle on herself."

"I doubt that," I said. "I tend to think she might have stayed in character. And by the way—you were right. This is *not* going to be a picnic."

author's note

THE LIVES THAT I HAVE ENDEAVORED TO PORTRAY IN THIS
book have been constructed primarily from interviews with
the following members of my family: my father, Denis
Haney, whom I interviewed extensively by telephone in the
year before his death as part of my research for an essay that
later became "Fair Shares for All," published in *Gourmet* in
2003; my mother, Katherine Latimer; my mother's sister,
Jacqueline Bush; my father's brother Raymond Haney; and
my sister, Joy Haney, with whom I was in constant communi-
cation, to the tune of hundreds of hours of conversation, from
the commencement of book development, in the summer of
2002, through the drafting of the final revision of the manu-
script in the summer of 2006.

I have also drawn on letters, postcards, and school reports
in my mother's possession; on photographs owned by my
mother, Jacqueline, and Joy; on photographs of my own; on
photographs inherited from my father; and on a video trans-
fer of home movies shot by my father between 1958 and 1964.

Last but not least, I have, of course, drawn on my own

memories and, in so doing, have made a point of focusing on the most indelible among them, on the ones to which I have found myself responding, as I wrote, not just emotionally but viscerally and physically, on the ones that still have the power to make me catch my breath. Most of those relate to crisis points in my family's history. That focus, in turn, has been central to the reconstruction of dialogue, all of which takes place in clearly remembered settings and at clearly remembered junctures, and reflects my own preoccupations—and those of the other participants in the dialogue, as I understood them—at the time.

This has been a relatively straightforward process with regard to conversations with my sister, who has provided the necessary corroboration. The reconstruction of talks with people who are now deceased, or with whom I have lost touch, is rooted in the clearest possible recall of the tenor of my association with them. For instance, my conversation with members of the Air Training Corps on my first parade night reflects, for dramatic purposes (and I consider this a perfectly legitimate ploy in the writing of memoir), both what I can remember of the conversation itself and what I came to know of the people involved—their foibles, their prejudices, their idiosyncrasies—during the three years I spent with them. I took the same approach in rendering my conversation with my girlfriend Helen on the night after my sister's wedding; the passage is essentially a dramatic re-creation (and condensation) of the real concerns that she and I had at that point in our relationship. In this sense, much of the dialogue in this memoir can be described as composite—or, perhaps more accurately, impressionistic.

All names of characters other than those of members of

my family have been changed, and at no point have I resorted to the use of composite characters. I strongly believe that, specifically in the context of memoir, no composite character can ever have the resonance of an individual character. I also believe that without that resonance no character can ring true.

ULTIMATELY, OF COURSE, no memory is an accurate reflection of reality, and it is, therefore, my firm conviction that no memoir can be—or should be—considered to have intrinsic documentary value. My own perceptions of the meaning of memory and of memoir can perhaps best be summed up in the principle that I have done my utmost to follow in the writing of this book: to make it the most accurate reflection possible of how things felt, not of how things were (because that is impossible). A memoir is an entirely subjective creation and perhaps, rather than being classified as a kind of nonfiction, is more properly subsumed within the realm of belles lettres.

acknowledgments

FIRST AND FOREMOST, I wish to thank Ruth Reichl, editor in chief of *Gourmet,* for her encouragement and support—and for having published the essay (also called "Fair Shares for All") from which this book grew. I must also thank five of my colleagues (past and present) at *Gourmet* for their patient and perceptive scrutiny of successive drafts of the book: Lillian Chou, Jane Daniels Lear, Nanette Maxim, Sofia Perez, and Elaine Richard. For assistance with scanning the photographs, I am grateful to Flavia Schepmans. My sister, Joy, has been my most acute nonprofessional critic.

ABOUT THE AUTHOR

JOHN HANEY was born in the London suburb
of Romford in 1954 and took a degree in classics
at the University of London in 1976. In 1982 he
moved to New York City, where he has now
been working in publishing for more than
twenty years. He is currently copy chief at
Gourmet magazine.

ABOUT THE TYPE

This book is set in Fournier, a typeface named
for Pierre Simon Fournier, the youngest son of
a French printing family. Pierre Simon first
studied watercolor painting, but became involved in type design through work that he did
for his eldest brother. Starting with engraving
woodblocks and large capitals, he later moved
on to fonts of type. In 1736 he began his own
foundry, and published the first version of his
point system the following year. He made several important contributions in the field of type
design; he cut and founded all the types himself,
pioneered the concepts of the type family, and is
said to have cut sixty thousand punches for 147
alphabets of his own design. He also created
new printers' ornaments.